What people are saying about

Take H

Harvey Kaye doesn't ju~~~ ~~~~~~~ history - he uses history to show exactly where we are today - and where we could take it. He has the wisdom of a sage, the passion of a prophet, and the intelligence of a true patriot. And he writes with compassion and guts.

John Fugelsang, Host of SiriusXM's *Tell Me Everything*

No one has ever loved a nation more or spanked it harder for straying from its premise than Harvey Kaye.

Norman Lear, TV/Writer and Producer and Founder of *People for the American Way*

Standing at the intersection of the past and the future stands Harvey Kaye, our great radical historian. Kaye practices his craft in the tradition of E.P. Thompson and Howard Zinn, turning our attention to neglected individuals, moments and messages that illuminate our understanding of who we have been and who we are. Yet, Harvey Kaye brings to his scholarship a distinctive academic commitment, as readers of this fine book will quickly and surely recognize. He believes, correctly, that our revolutionary past provides the truest evidence that another world is possible.

John Nichols, *The Nation*

Harvey Kaye is our essential and always engaging guide to owning our progressive history. America has a rich progressive social-democratic history that has been obscured by the Right and all too often ignored by the Left. But now, as Bernie Sanders leads a social-democratic presidential campaign, we have an opportunity to assert a new politics. Whatever your politics are, you need to know this history and argument.

Michael Brooks, *The Michael Brooks Show*

Progressives have often allowed the right to co-opt American values and history, distorting them for their own use. This collection is a call to arms for progressives to reclaim the mantle of patriotism and resist right wing authoritarianism with the only thing that has ever worked, a pro-worker progressive agenda. Harvey Kaye does the essential work of explaining why now is the time to be in the words of FDR: "fairly radical for a generation."

Krystal Ball, *Rising on Hill.TV*

Harvey Kaye does it again, with a brilliant, historically-grounded, deeply insightful prescription to our nation's ills – grounded in what we already know works! Read, share, and act!

Thom Hartmann, *The Thom Hartmann Show*

Take Hold of Our History

Make America Radical Again

Take Hold of Our History

Make America Radical Again

Harvey J. Kaye

Winchester, UK
Washington, USA

JOHN HUNT PUBLISHING

First published by Zero Books, 2020
Zero Books is an imprint of John Hunt Publishing Ltd., No. 3 East St., Alresford,
Hampshire SO24 9EE, UK
office@jhpbooks.com
www.johnhuntpublishing.com
www.zero-books.net

For distributor details and how to order please visit the 'Ordering' section on our website.

ISBN: 978 1 78904 355 6
978 1 78904 356 3 (ebook)
Library of Congress Control Number: 2019905185

A CIP catalogue record for this book is available from the British Library.

Design: Stuart Davies

UK: Printed and bound by CPI Group (UK) Ltd, Croydon, CR0 4YY
US: Printed and bound by Thomson-Shore, 7300 West Joy Road, Dexter, MI 48130

We operate a distinctive and ethical publishing philosophy in
all areas of our business, from our global network of authors to
production and worldwide distribution.

Contents

Dedicated to my friends and mentors
Bill Moyers and Bernie Weisberger
and to my grandson (aka "grandboy")
Toby Gareth Imler

ALSO BY HARVEY J. KAYE

AUTHOR

The British Marxist Historians
The Powers of The Past
The Education of Desire
"Why Do Ruling Classes Fear History?" and Other Questions
Thomas Paine: Firebrand of Revolution
Are We Good Citizens?
Thomas Paine and the Promise of America
The Fight for the Four Freedoms

EDITOR

History, Classes, and Nation-States: Selected Writings of V.G.
Kiernan
The Face of the Crowd: Selected Essays of George Rudé
Poets, Politics, and the People: Selected Essays of V.G. Kiernan
E.P. Thompson: Critical Perspectives (with Keith McClelland)
The American Radical (with Mari Jo Buhle and Paul Buhle)
Imperialism and Its Contradictions: Selected Essays of V.G. Kiernan

The basic story in the American past, the only story ultimately worth the telling, is the story of the struggle between the creative and the frustrating elements in the democratic adventure...

Every generation needs to know what it is fighting against, whom it is fighting with, what it is fighting for...

At critical stages in the struggle with plutocratic control, there have been upsurges of democratic strength...

To me the most important development in the radical movement does not lie in its replacement of capitalism for fascism as the tyrant-symbol, nor even in its Popular Front tactic... It lies in its rediscovery of the past.... We have looked back to history, and we have found a usable past – and one that we can call ours. And such a discovery of the past, if it is sincere and deeply experienced, may set us on our own path to the future.

– Max Lerner, It Is Later than You Think:
The Need for a Militant Democracy (1938)

Introduction

On December 1, 1862, in the midst of the Civil War, just weeks before he was to issue the Emancipation Proclamation, President Abraham Lincoln delivered his Annual Message to Congress. Lincoln firmly believed that the United States had an historic responsibility to demonstrate to the world that people can govern themselves, make equal rights not just a self-evident truth but a manifest one, and create a political and economic order in which working people, both white and black, are not compelled to bow to anyone, neither aristocrats nor capitalists. Empowered by tens of thousands of black slaves who were already liberating themselves from bondage by escaping to the Union lines, and increasingly confident that the majority of his fellow Americans would recognize the truth of what he was saying, Lincoln closed his address by calling on them to see that the time had come to remember who they were and what that demanded. He told them that to save the nation and all that it represented, they must live up to the nation's declared revolutionary purpose and promise and act to radically enhance American freedom by bringing an end to slavery:

> Fellow-citizens, *we* cannot escape history… The fiery trial through which we pass, will light us down, in honor or dishonor, to the latest generation. We *say* we are for the Union. The world will not forget that we say this. We know how to save the Union. The world knows we do know how to save it. *We – even* we here – hold the power, and bear the responsibility. In *giving* freedom to the *slave*, we *assure* freedom to the *free* – honorable alike in what we give, and what we preserve. We shall nobly save, or meanly lose, the last best hope of earth.

We too cannot escape history… Our own struggle to save the

1

nation and the promise it proclaims has begun. Finally, after more than forty years of fear driven class-war and culture-war campaigns against the democratic achievements of generations, the hard-won rights of workers, women, and people of color, and the very memory of how they were secured – and now, both in the wake of the election debacle of 2016, which gave the presidency to the corrupt, mendacious, racist, sexist, and treacherous demagogue Donald Trump and continued control of Congress to the formerly conservative but increasingly reactionary Republican party, *and* in the face of intensified class and culture war campaigns – We the People have come not only to recognize that American democratic life is in jeopardy, but also to mobilize in hopes of saving it. Millions of us have rallied to the "Resistance" and expressed our democratic fears and desires in action – in the historic Women's March and March for Our Lives of young people; the protests, demonstrations, and legal actions to defend the lives and rights of immigrants and refugees; the #MeToo movement to combat sexual assault and harassment; the massive teachers' strikes for higher pay and better funding of public schools in states red and blue; *and* the enthusiastic canvassing and campaigning for a "Blue Wave" to win back Congress in the 2018 midterm elections. But resistance is not enough.

The time has come for us to remember who we are and what that demands. The time has come for us to embrace our radical history. The history of how a generation of Americans high and low and in all their diversity not only turned their colonial rebellion into a war for independence, but also imbued American life – whether they all intended it or not – with radical imperative and impulse by declaring a revolutionary promise of freedom, equality, and democracy for all. The history of how generations of radicals and reformers served as the prophetic memory of that promise *and* how generations of ordinary men and women, native-born and immigrant, struggled to make real the right to "life, liberty, and the pursuit of happiness" and to expand not only the *We* in We the People, but also the powers of the people. And most especially in view of the crises we ourselves face, the history of how our greatest generations confronted and prevailed over the forces that threatened to destroy the nation and bury its revolutionary promise in the 1770s, 1860s, and 1930s and 1940s (not to mention the 1960s), by acting to make the United States – both inspired by Washington, Lincoln, and FDR *and* pushing them to go further than they might otherwise have gone – radically freer, more equal, and more democratic than ever before. The time has come to take hold of that history and make America radical again.

I have titled this collection of my speeches and essays *Take Hold of Our History: Make America Radical Again* for reasons that will become obvious. And yet I cannot help but confess that if I had had to title it otherwise, I would have been sorely tempted to use – with full attribution – the title Max Lerner gave to his 1938 work, It Is Later than You Think: The Need for a Militant Democracy. While it may not seem so, the crisis we face is no less demanding of action, urgent action, than that which confronted his generation. And just as his generation did – indeed, our great advantage is that we are the children and grandchildren of his generation – we must save American democratic life for our children by radically enhancing it.

The chapters that follow were written over the course of the past ten years, from the outset of the Barack Obama presidency to the early months of Donald Trump's occupation of the White House. Years in which Americans not only continued to endure the class war from above by corporate interests and their conservative and neoliberal political champions, but also suffered and in all too many cases never really recovered from the Great Recession. Years in which many of us began, after long silence, to chant *This is what democracy looks like!* and to challenge

– first, in the Wisconsin Rising and Occupy encampments and, then, in the Fight for $15, anti-pipeline and anti-fracking protests, North Carolina Moral Monday Movement, Chicago Teachers' Strike, and Black Lives Matter – the unrelenting class war from above and the devastation and injustices it was wreaking. Years in which a well-funded Tea Party movement pushed and then pulled the Republicans all the further to the right, and a neoliberal-dominated Democratic party tragically squandered Americans' emerging democratic insurgencies. Years in which democratic-left politicians, activists, and public intellectuals, apparently haunted by the worst of American experience – and sorely ignoring the work of a generation of historians revealing the tragic, ironic, *and yet progressive* history of the United States – turned away, if not ran, from the past and failed to articulate and advance a story that would engage our shared democratic anxieties and longings, encourage our persistent democratic hopes and aspirations, *and* empower our renewed democratic energies and agencies. Years that engendered disappointment, frustration, anger, and resentment and ultimately led, with the help of the Electoral College (and quite possibly Russian hackers and social-media agents), to the Trump presidency, the GOP stranglehold on Congress, *and* a conservative majority on the Supreme Court.

Notably, while all of the pieces collected here were to be published, some originated as speeches and others as essays and reviews. A few were prepared specifically for student and academic audiences; others, for gatherings of labor and left comrades; and still others for speaking to as many of my fellow citizens as I could reach in a room, on the airwaves, or online. They notably vary in tone and tenor, as well. Some were authored to educate listeners and readers to America's radical story; some, to assail conservatives and/or chastise liberals and leftists; others, to express and register our shared outrage, articulate our persistent hopes, and hearten our democratic determination and action; and yet others, to publicly recall and commemorate Americans revolutionary, radical, and progressive who struggled to enhance American freedom, equality, and democracy. But as varied as these chapters are in those respects, together they can be read and heard as a manifesto – a call to action – a call to Americans to embrace our radical history.

They call on us – especially politicians, political activists, and public intellectuals of the democratic left – to stop running from the past. They call on us not only to reject the tales and narratives of the right intended to make us forget who we are, what we have accomplished, *and* what we might yet accomplish, but also to reach beyond the all too often cynicism-inducing debunking and deconstruction of the left and to reclaim the truly radical history of America – a history that remains, for all of the exploitation, oppression, and injustices that have marked the nation's experience, and continue to do so, a progressive, promising, and inspiring one.

They call on us to outfit ourselves with that history and to speak historically to our fellow Americans – to engage their democratic yearnings, encourage their democratic aspirations, and empower their democratic agencies. They call on us to remind Americans that whether we are native-born or newly-arrived we are the heirs to both America's revolutionary purpose and promise *and* the struggles and achievements of generations of Americans in all their diversity who fought to make America *America*. And they call on us to enable them to recognize that if we are to save American democratic life from the crises and forces that threaten to destroy it today, we must not only resist them and defend and protect it, but, just as our forebears did, defeat them and radically enhance it.

Finally, they call on us to remind ourselves and our fellow Americans that, no less than those who came before us, we are radicals at heart – and that the time has come to take hold of our history and make America radical again.

1

Americans Should Embrace Their Radical History

*I delivered this speech/resolution at the invitation of the Yale
Political Union (YPU) on February 25, 2009. Composed of
student political groups from across the political spectrum,
the YPU is the oldest collegiate debating society in America.
Students responded enthusiastically both for and against, but
my resolution passed by a margin of two to one. Originally
posted at OurFuture.org in 2009, Moyers and Company
published it anew on October 8, 2014.*

In his 1939 book – *It Is Later Than You Think: The Need for a Militant
Democracy* – progressive writer Max Lerner argued that "The
basic story in the American past, the only story ultimately worth
the telling, is the story of the struggle between the creative and
the frustrating elements in the American democratic adventure."

With Lerner's words in mind, I now move that *AMERICANS
SHOULD EMBRACE THEIR RADICAL HISTORY*. And to second
the resolution, I call upon a voice from 1930, one of America's
finest voices, the voice of Franklin Delano Roosevelt, a man
destined to become the greatest president of the twentieth
century.

Looking back on ten years of conservative-Republican
presidential administration and what they had wrought – an
intensifying economic crisis and spreading human misery that
would come to be known as the Great Depression – FDR, who
was then the Governor of New York State, said: "There is no
question in my mind that it is time for the country to become
fairly radical for a generation."

And do we not see what Roosevelt saw then?

We have experienced three decades of conservative ascendance and power. Three decades, in which well-funded conservative movements, and ambitious and determined political and economic elites, secured power and subordinated the public good to corporate priorities, enriched the rich at the expense of working people, hollowed out the nation's economy and public infrastructure, and harnessed religion and patriotism to the pursuit of power and wealth. In short, we have endured thirty years of rightwing political reaction and class war from above intended to undo or undermine the progressive advances of the 1930s and 1960s.

Plus, if all that were not enough, we have suffered eight years of a presidency – the presidency of George W. Bush – marked not only by the tragedies of 9/11, war in Iraq, Hurricane Katrina, *and* the collapse of an interstate highway bridge in Minnesota, but also by assaults on our civil liberties, the denigration of human rights, breaches in the wall separating church and state, tax cuts for the wealthy, a campaign to privatize Social Security, continued corporate attacks on labor unions, and the pursuit of a politics of fear and loathing – all of which has not only led us to the brink of economic and social catastrophe, but also effectively placed the American dream and the nation's exceptional purpose and promise under siege.

We clearly see the consequences of conservative rule or, more accurately, *misrule* – not to mention liberal deference to it.

I therefore urge this assembly to resolve that, "We Americans should embrace our radical history" – and as FDR himself averred – "make the nation radical for a generation."

I do so not only because the circumstances we confront demand a radical response, but also because to do otherwise would be to deny who we are. Our shared past calls on us to do so. Our own historical longings urge us to do so. And Americans yet to be await our determination in doing so.

Let us start by recalling our history and reminding ourselves who we are – a by no means simple or easy task. For as ruling classes have been ever wont to do, America's own powers that be have regularly sought to control the telling of the past in favor of controlling the present and the future.

I could take you through a long list of New Right initiatives – from Ronald Reagan to George W. Bush – intended to determine the shape and content of American memory, consciousness, and imagination. But let's just consider the popular little volume and video – *Rediscovering God in America* – authored and produced by one of America's smartest and most prominent conservatives, former Speaker of the House Newt Gingrich. Therein, Gingrich, a Ph.D. in History, takes us on a walking tour of Washington D.C. – a walking tour in which he guides us around the Mall to discuss both the monuments and the figures they memorialize.

Sounds nice, right? But there's more to it. Along the way Gingrich presents a narrative of U.S. history that attributes America's founding, survival, *and* progress to Divine will, to our unceasing faith in and devotion to God, *and* to our having sustained God's and religion's presence in the public square.

Fair enough, you might say. However, after bizarrely and vehemently warning that "There is no attack on American culture more destructive and more historically dishonest than the secular left's relentless effort to drive God out of the public square," Gingrich not only discounts or ignores the fact that most of the leading Founders were deists not Christians and that – in one of the most revolutionary acts of the age – they wrote a "Godless Constitution" which provided for the separation of church and state. He also somehow neglects to mention that those originally most determined to assure that separation included not just the usual suspects, but also Christian evangelicals.

Nevertheless – with all due respect to God and the faithful among us – we must remember who we are, for as Wilson Carey McWilliams proffered twenty-five years ago: "A people's memory sets the measure of its political freedom. The old times give us models and standards by which to judge our time; what has been suggests what might have been and may yet be. Remembering lifts us out of bondage to the present, and political recollection calls us back from the specialization of everyday existence, allowing us to see ourselves as a people sharing a heritage and a public life."

So let us not forget that we are the descendants of Revolutionaries – of men and women who, inspired by an immigrant working-class pamphleteer, Thomas Paine, through words such as "The sun never shined on a cause of greater worth," "We have it in our power to begin the world over again," *and* "These are the times that try men's souls," not only turned their colonial rebellion into a war for independence, but also transformed themselves into a nation of citizens, not subjects; endowed their new nation with exceptional purpose and promise; and launched a world-historic experiment in extending and deepening freedom, equality, and democracy.

Let us not forget that we are the descendants of generations of radicals – of men and women, native-born and immigrant, who struggled not only to realize the American dream, but also to expand the "We" in "We the People." Recognizing the contradictions between the nation's ideals and realities – and rejecting the notion that the American experiment had reached its limits – evangelicals, workingmen's advocates, freethinkers, slaves and abolitionists, suffragists, populists, labor unionists, socialists, anarchists, and progressives, respectively, dissented from their established churches; pressed for the rights of workingmen; insisted on the separation of church and state; resisted their masters; demanded an end to slavery; campaigned for the equality of women; challenged the power of property and officialdom; *and together* made the nineteenth century an age not only of growth, expansion, conflict, and the accumulation of capital, but also of militant democracy.

And let us not forget that we are the children and grandchildren of America's most progressive generation, the men and women who confronted the Great Depression and the Second World War – the men and women who not only made the "We" in "We the People" all the more inclusive, but also subjected big business to public account and regulation; empowered government to address the needs of working people; organized labor unions; fought for their rights; established Social Security; expanded the nation's public infrastructure; refurbished its physical environment; and defeated the tyrannies of German fascism and Japanese imperialism.

And you yourselves are the children of a generation who – for all of our many faults and failings – marched for civil rights, pursued the vision of a Great Society, challenged cultural prohibitions and inhibitions, pushed open institutional doors for women and people of color, and protested an imperial war in Southeast Asia. Admittedly, we made mistakes, regrettable mistakes. But we also made America better and more promising in the process.

Finally, let us never forget that we are the descendants of Americans who – confronting seemingly overwhelming crises in the 1770s, 1860s, and 1930s and '40s – not only rescued the United States from division, defeat, and devastation, but also succeeded, against great odds and expectations, in extending and deepening freedom, equality, and democracy further than they had ever reached before.

Still, I do not argue that we "should embrace our radical history" merely because we owe it to past generations to do so – though that in itself is a good, strong, and compelling reason to do so.

I further contend that we should embrace our radical history, because we owe it to ourselves – and, ultimately, to Americans yet to come – to do so

As our greatest democratic poet Walt Whitman rightly saw it: "There must be continual additions to our great experiment of how much liberty society will bear."

Or, even better, as the progressive journalist Henry Demarest Lloyd put it a century ago – in words that I believe you will immediately grasp: "The price of liberty is something more than eternal vigilance. There must also be eternal advance. We can save the rights we have inherited from our fathers only by winning new ones to bequeath our children."

Those words do speak to you – don't they? *You know why?* Because you are Americans – and no less so than any previous generation of Americans, you – all of us – remain radicals at heart.

Yes, the likes of *Newsweek* editor Jon Meacham tell us that "America remains a center-right nation." And yes, former Reagan speechwriter and now *Wall Street Journal* columnist Peggy Noonan has very graciously reminded us that our newly-inaugurated President Obama "would be most unwise to rouse the sleeping giant that is conservatism." But such talk ignores or denies what we ourselves feel and have been feeling for some time...

While we may not yet fully recognize it, we ourselves continue to feel the radical impulse and democratic imperative that generations of Americans, through their struggles, passed on to us – or better said, endowed or imbued us with. Truly, we never stopped feeling them.

Ask yourselves this: Why was it that in the midst of the seemingly most conservative political era since the 1920s, Americans passionately sought to recall, honor, celebrate, *and* engage America's most revolutionary and progressive generations – the nation's Founders *and* the so-called Greatest Generation and its greatest leader, FDR?

Most of you are probably too young to remember the mid-1990s explosion of interest in the likes of Washington, Franklin, Adams, Jefferson, Madison, Hamilton, and yes, Paine – an explosion of interest that editors and academics alike somewhat dismissively referred to as "Founders' Chic."

And you may also be too young to remember the even grander explosion of interest in FDR and the young men and women of the Great Depression who went on to fight the Second World War – an explosion of interest that turned books like Tom Brokaw's *The Greatest Generation* into bestsellers and films like Steven Spielberg's *Saving Private Ryan* into blockbuster hits; that made television series such as HBO's *Band of Brothers* and Ken Burns' *The War* major events; and that instigated innumerable popular gatherings around the country. Indeed, an explosion of interest that led us to erect two new grand monuments in the very heart of the nation's capital: one to Franklin Roosevelt and the other to the 16,000,000 veterans of World War II.

But even if you do remember those developments, you may not have critically considered what they represented. And you would not have been alone in not doing so.

Consider the phenomenal interest in the Greatest Generation and its greatest leader. While commentators marveled at its scale and intensity, they never seemed to grasp the most profound meaning of it all. Discussing the New Deal as merely a massive program of economic recovery and the Second World War as just a series of vast military struggles – and describing Americans' expressions of admiration and affection as if it were all one big farewell party – mainstream media folk never really appreciated or acknowledged either the radical-democratic achievements of the men and women of the 1930s and 1940s *or* the radical-democratic anxieties and yearnings that motivated the popular desire to thank, honor, and celebrate the generation that was passing away.

In fact, many a conservative – after decrying that FDR didn't even deserve a monument – used the interest in and admiration for the Greatest Generation as an opportunity to attack the Sixties Generation for challenging the nation's political and cultural order and opposing the war in Vietnam. And sadly enough, leftists did little better. They either belittled the attention to the wartime generation as nothing more than nostalgia, media hype, and the commercialization of the past *or* – in a somewhat paranoid fashion – charged that government and media were orchestrating a campaign to eradicate the nation's "Vietnam syndrome" in favor of new "imperial adventures."

Such critics – right and left – never really considered the connection between what Americans were experiencing *and* what they might actually have been trying to say and do. We, however, should not fail to consider it.

Recall that in November 1992, Americans – despite the nation's victories in the very long Cold War and the very brief Gulf War – turned out the Republican incumbent George H.W. Bush in favor of Democrat Bill Clinton, the presidential candidate who not only emphasized "change," but also promised to address the needs of middle- and working-class families by, among other things, investing in the nation's already crumbling public infrastructure, protecting the environment, and establishing a system of universal national health care.

Of course, if Americans truly were expecting renewed liberalism, they were to be sadly disappointed, for Clinton quickly betrayed those who had worked to place him in office by making his first priority the passage of the North American Free Trade Agreement, an initiative proposed by Republicans and promoted by big corporations.

And we know what happened next. In the wake of NAFTA's passage and the death of the promised progressive endeavors, Republicans, led by Newt Gingrich, took control of both houses of Congress for the first time in forty years.

Change and growth ensued, but not always or exactly the sort hoped for in 1992. In addition to learning of "ethnic cleansing" in the Balkans and genocidal civil wars in Africa, Americans witnessed accelerating globalization, persistent corporate "downsizing," the further deregulation of capital and privatization of public goods and services, the steady erosion of the nation's industrial base and decay of its public infrastructure, continuing assaults on labor, increasing concentration of wealth, intensifying material insecurities, the termination of Aid to Families with Dependent Children, the growth of illegal immigration, virulent "culture wars," the emergence of rightwing militias, foreign and domestic terrorist attacks, burnings of black churches, killings at family-planning clinics, the impeachment of a president, and a quite possibly stolen presidential election in 2000.

Never get nostalgic about the 1990s!

Politicians and pundits of every sort described Americans as deeply divided, angry, and cynical, and Americans surely had substantial cause to feel that way. And yet they did not – at least not in the fashion asserted by all the media talk and images.

More serious studies showed that while Americans felt anxious, resentful, and even pessimistic, they not only continued to subscribe to both the "American creed of liberty, equality, and democracy" *and* the "melting pot theory of national identity." They also continued to believe – even while recognizing that Americans had far from always lived up to them – that those very ideals and aspirations defined what it meant to be an American.

In other words, Americans still possessed a shared understanding of and commitment to the nation's historic purpose and promise – though they did wonder seriously about its prospects and possibilities.

What politicians and pundits missed – or tried to obscure – about the popular desire and effort to reconnect with the Founders and the Greatest Generation was that Americans were doing exactly what Americans have always done when they sense that the American dream and the nation's historic purpose and promise are in jeopardy.

Almost instinctively, they were looking back – back to those who originally and most powerfully expressed what it meant to be an American – most particularly to those who, facing crises themselves, made the United States radically freer, more equal, and more democratic in the process.

Even after thirty years of conservative and corporate rule – even after concerted efforts to make us forget, or at least confuse us about our history and what it has to say to us – we, too, not only yearn to redeem America's purpose and promise. We also find ourselves looking back and reaching out to America's Revolutionary and radical pasts. The task however – a task made all the more urgent by the crisis we face – is to embrace it. And perhaps we are not so far from doing just that...

In fact, maybe the resolution before us is not as fantastic as it seems... For if we look closely, we might well see that Americans are already reaching out to grab hold of and embrace their radical history. We might well see that instead of simply saying "We Americans should embrace our radical history," we should actually be leaning into it and saying: "*YES*, We Americans *should embrace* our radical history." Or – to quote a recently popular refrain – "Yes, we can."

Now don't get me wrong. I am not calling Barack Obama a radical. I'll leave that to Rush Limbaugh or Sarah Palin (or to her smarter body-double, Tina Fey). Nevertheless, something critical, something progressive – and possibly even radical – seems to be happening.

Think back five weeks – to January 20 – to the inauguration of our new president. Inaugurations are always historic occasions, especially when one party replaces another. But this time it was historic in an even grander sense, for Americans had elected a black man to their nation's highest office.

Of course, racism persists. But the day that Barack Obama took the oath of office was not simply a break with the past. It was truly a day of transcendence.

Looking from the Mall up to the Capitol – either standing there in the cold or watching on television – Americans, not only

African Americans, but all Americans, had reason to take pride and even shed tears of joy.

And yet, perhaps there was even more going on than that – that is, more than the talking-head politicians, pundits, and presidential scholars pointed out to us.

Here's what I mean...

Shift the vantage point and look out on the Mall from the Capitol as our new president did. Now if Newt Gingrich – or the Reverend Rick Warren – were talking to us, they would tell us that we were witnessing the American people assembled together in the presence of the Almighty.

But I saw something else that day – and maybe many of you did, too. I saw something that made me think that as much as Obama's ascendance to the presidency represented a radical break with the past, it also represented something oh-so-very American, and yet again, in that very way, something also truly radical and truly promising.

I saw two million Americans gathered together amidst monuments and memorials that testify not so much to God's beneficence – or, at least, not to that alone – but all the more to our persistent aspirations and perennial efforts to extend and deepen freedom, equality, and democracy.

I saw two million Americans – in all their wonderful diversity – celebrating their democratic lives, peering into the future with hope and expectation, *and* pressing up against monuments and memorials that render nothing less than a grand narrative of revolution and radicalism.

There they were – there we were – standing beneath a monument to a man who led a revolutionary army; chaired a constitutional convention that announced to the world that here in the United States "We the People" rule; *and* served as the first president of a pioneering, democratic republic.

There they were, standing before a memorial to the man who wrote the words declaring "all men are created equal."

There they were, standing in front of a monument to the man who – leading the Union through a bloody Civil War – proclaimed a "new birth of freedom" and called on his fellow citizens to devote themselves to assuring that "government of the people, by the people, for the people, shall not perish from the earth."

There they were, standing by a memorial to the man who – in the very toughest of times – articulated our grandest and most radical aspirations in terms of four essential freedoms: "Freedom of speech and expression... Freedom of worship... Freedom from want... Freedom from Fear..."

And closer in, there they were at a memorial to our parents and grandparents, Americans who, in their many millions, fought and labored for those Four Freedoms.

One could almost hear Marian Anderson singing *God Bless America* and Martin Luther King, Jr., pronouncing "I Have a Dream," from the steps of the Lincoln Memorial.

And if that were not enough, we actually heard our new president essentially calling them all forth to stand with us. He spoke of our revolutionary and radical pasts. He spoke of America's continuing purpose and promise. And he spoke of what *we* needed to do by reciting the words that Washington ordered read to his troops on that cold and fateful Christmas eve in 1776 – words of Thomas Paine from his revolutionary pamphlet, *The Crisis*: "Let it be told to the future world... that in the depth of winter, when nothing but hope and virtue could survive ... that the city and the country, alarmed at one common danger, came forth to meet [it]."

Again, I am not saying that Obama himself is a radical – Hell, he used Paine's words, but never mentioned Paine's name!

But really, the point isn't whether Obama is or isn't a radical. It's that we ourselves need to be.

Only then might *we* make him the great democratic president that we require. And even more crucially, only then – in the best of our traditions – might we redeem America's purpose and promise and make an even greater nation for ourselves and for those who follow us.

We have much to do. In addition to repairing the damage to the Constitution of the past eight years, we must enact the Employee Free Choice Act, establish universal health care, re-appropriate the wealth appropriated from working people, invest in new technologies, refurbish our public spaces and national infrastructure, democratize corporations, and pursue a New Deal on immigration.

Propelled by the memory and legacy of those who came before us, the yearnings and aspirations we ourselves feel, and the responsibility we have to those yet to come, we can pursue not only recovery and reconstruction, but also the making of a freer, more equal, and more democratic America.

So – leaning into it and saying it as I should have said it to begin with – I call on this House to join me in resolving that "We Americans *SHOULD EMBRACE* our radical history."

2

Obama is no FDR...

Originally posted at Dissent On-Line, October 20, 2010.

Two years ago, it looked like we were on the verge of a new Age of Roosevelt. Today, however, with elections fast approaching, we talk not of FDR in the 1930s, but of Bill Clinton in 1994 and Jimmy Carter in 1980 – the possibility, if not the likelihood, that the Democrats will lose one or both houses of Congress this November and, in 2012, the White House itself.

The lines are being written and rehearsed. "Forget FDR. America is a center-right nation... Americans are essentially conservatives... Obama went too far, too fast, and asked too much of Americans."

Bullshit. Obama didn't ask too much of Americans. He asked *too little* of them.

In 2008-2009 magazines popular and political ran cover stories projecting Obama as possibly the Second Coming of FDR. Liberals had great expectations – and conservatives, grand fears – that big wins that November would lead both to the launching of a "new New Deal" to tackle America's unfolding economic crisis, deepening inequality, and continuing industrial and infrastructural decay *and* to the making of a new politics that would propel progressive initiatives for years to come. Indeed, in the wake of eight years of Bush, many of us were looking forward to redeeming FDR's vision of the Four Freedoms: "Freedom of speech, Freedom of worship, Freedom from want, Freedom from fear."

Nancy Pelosi herself had said that she had three words to offer in response to Republican assertions that the Democrats had run out of ideas: "Franklin Delano Roosevelt." And following Obama's and the Democrats' victories in November 2008 – and the Republicans' retreat into Dixie – pundits and pols imagined, at the least, that just as Roosevelt and the New Dealers had strengthened their hold on Congress in the 1934 midterm elections, so too would Obama and the Democrats buck history and gain seats in the midterm elections of 2010. However, all we hear now is talk such as "Why Has He Fallen Short?" and "The Sweep: How did it come to this?"

Strangely enough, Obama himself, the man who wrote *The Audacity of Hope*, preached Hope and Change, and inspired so many of his fellow citizens to believe "Yes we can," seems shocked by the prevailing apathy and disinterest. Surely, he asks: Didn't I act swiftly to stabilize the nation's financial system? Didn't I secure passage of a massive economic stimulus package to revive the economy and save millions of jobs that would otherwise have been lost? And didn't I enact legislation that would guarantee health care to millions who were not previously covered? Where, he must wonder, is the love, admiration, and support that Roosevelt garnered..?

Critics to the President's left argue that Obama was too eager to cut deals with capitalists – with Wall Street and the health insurance and pharmaceutical industries – and too ready to compromise with Republicans. Others, more centrist folk, such as John Judis in the *New Republic* (September 2), Michael Tomasky in the *New York Review of Books* (October 28), and Jonathan Alter in his book *The Promise*, contend, respectively, that Obama failed to speak like a populist, failed to offer "broad and convincing arguments," and failed to clarify and sustain his message.

Liberal defenders of the President reply that FDR, too, cut deals and made compromises. They point out that in his famous First Hundred Days he deferred to big business and big landowners in the National Industrial Recovery Act (NIRA) and Agricultural Adjustment Act (AAA) and that to win passage of Social Security he allowed reactionary Dixiecrats to exclude agricultural and domestic workers – mostly African Americans – from its provisions. Moreover, Obama's guardians note that Roosevelt didn't even create the Works Progress Administration (WPA) and enact the National Labor Relations Act (NLRA – aka the Wagner Act) and Social Security Act until 1935.

All true. But critics and defenders alike ignore the most crucial thing that Roosevelt did. From the very outset in 1933, he actively engaged American working people and young people in both the struggles and the labors of recovery, reconstruction, and reform. The NIRA and the AAA, respectively, enabled working men and women to organize AFL unions and Midwestern family farmers to create boards to shape the process of economic recovery in industry and agriculture, and also led the way to the Wagner Act (with its federal NLRB) and the formation from the bottom up of the CIO, as well as to a host of popular rural development initiatives, including rural electrification. The Civilian Conservation Corps (CCC) recruited young men to plant trees, fight soil erosion, and build not only parks and recreation areas but also themselves both physically and mentally in the process and pioneered the way to the establishment in 1935 of the National Youth Administration (NYA), which enabled millions of boys and girls and young men and women, white and black, to advance their educations and improve American public and economic life. And when jobs didn't "grow" as fast as they were needed, FDR and New-Dealer Harry Hopkins created temporary jobs through the Federal Emergency Relief Administration (FERA) and the Civil Works Administration (CWA), which paved the way to setting up the WPA in 1935.

Americans – working people and young people in all their diversity, the folks who voted for Obama in November 2008 – were ready to act. You could see it at the Inauguration in January 2009 and you could feel it in labor councils, community centers, and college classrooms across the country.

However, there was no call, no empowerment, no mobilization.

Despite his promises on the campaign trail, Obama never pushed to enact the Employee Free Choice Act (EFCA) that would have challenged and better enabled labor to organize the millions who wanted organizing. For all of his professions, he never instituted major national service initiatives to afford programs, internships, and apprenticeships for young graduates to remake America and themselves. And for all of his preaching, he never rallied citizens to mobilize and fill the public squares and spaces – before the Tea Partiers did – to fight for a national health care system that would not just control prices and cover everyone, but also encourage further progressive campaigns to extend and deepen freedom, equality, and democracy.

Once sworn in, Obama failed to energize his fellow citizens and engage them in the process of renewal. Instead of harnessing the hopes and aspirations he had encouraged to help him win the presidency, he left them hanging. And two years later Americans feel let down and detached. We are not conservatives – other than in the sense that we want to conserve and build upon the good and the great that is America. We remain progressives at heart – but now, it seems, hopelessly so.

3

This is What Democracy Looks Like!

Originally posted at Huffington Post, February 28, 2011

JUSTICE – GOVERNMENT – LEGISLATION — LIBERTY. Choose the order in which to recite them. Those are themes of the four murals that adorn the Capitol Rotunda in Madison, Wisconsin and surround the throngs of citizens who have gathered for many days now to protest and, we hope, block the passage of the anti-labor, indeed, anti-democratic Budget Repair Bill proposed by Governor Scott Walker – a bill that not only slashes public workers' incomes, but also strips them/us of their/ our democratic rights to bargain collectively.

On Friday my wife Lorna and I decided, quite suddenly, to go down to Madison. We made the 300-mile roundtrip drive on Friday to help bolster our fellow citizens on the eve of the big events on Saturday; to register our anger at the Republican-dominated Assembly's shameful passage of the bill (the Republican-dominated Senate remains "filibustered" with Senate Democrats holding out in Illinois); *and* to renew our own spirits in the face of the media's inadequate coverage and misrepresentation of what is at stake.

Arriving mid-afternoon, we went straight to the "unionized" Concourse Hotel, where Wisconsin's labor organizations have their "war rooms" set up. There we got caught up on developments and picked up "WI red" AFL-CIO signs bearing a blue map of the state in the shape of a fist and the words STAND WITH WISCONSIN. Informed and equipped, we headed up to the Capitol.

It was a chilly 20-degree afternoon, but it was bright outside and one had the sense that the state's motto "FORWARD!" still mattered. Police officers, drawn from cities and towns around the state, guarded entrances and patrolled counter-clockwise to the marchers. But at least for now, they too were smiling. In fact, to show their solidarity with the protestors, the Wisconsin Professional Police Association responded to reports that the governor's office was planning to close the Capitol that night and clear sleeping protestors from its halls by announcing that some of its own union brothers and sisters were going to sleep in the building along with protestors. (As one of my colleagues put it, most hopefully: "Oh boy, the cops are coming to Madison for a sleepover. Does this mean they are in bed with the demonstrators?")

After one full circle, we went into the Capitol building. It's a gorgeous place, not unlike the Capitol in D.C. And it was made all the more gorgeous and welcoming by the presence of the hundreds, no thousands, of our fellow citizens occupying nearly every corner of the place. Posters adorned the walls and banisters, and noise – good noise of citizens' voices and young drummers – reverberated throughout. And yet, somehow everything remained "Wisconsin clean."

Moving with others into the Rotunda area, beneath the great dome, I could not help but look up and around – and what I saw and heard made me tearful, joyfully so: Throngs of people, the four murals above, the many signs that read "Beam Scotty Up," "Scott Walker is a Weasel, Not a Badger," "Forward! Never Backwards!" "The People Own this BLDG, the Kochs Own Walker," "I'm Sorry if My Rights are an Inconvenience for You," and "Stop the Class War Against Workers!," and the banners of diverse Wisconsin unions.

At the center of it all was the "People's Microphone" (smartly managed by a group of young people whom I assumed were members of UW-Madison's Graduate Assistants Union). There, one-by-one, people young and old spoke: students, Wisconsin unionists, and labor delegations from around the USA. Teenagers spoke in support of their teachers and parents. Workers of every trade decried the Republicans' so-called Budget Repair Bill and the corruption of democracy by billionaires such as the Koch Brothers; recounted how their own parents and grandparents struggled to organize unions and secure their democratic rights; and declared their determination to fight on... And folks from New York, Florida, Michigan, and points west registered their own unions' solidarity with Wisconsin.

Each little speech garnered rousing cheers – and regularly everyone broke into "Kill the bill!" But just as regularly, and just as enthusiastically and tunefully, we all sang out with "This is what Democracy looks like!" – accompanied by young drummers beating out the rhythm on large white plastic containers.

Voices never spoke hatefully. But they expressed outrage – an outrage built up over thirty years in which the rich have become extraordinarily richer and working people poorer, in which livelihoods and industries have been destroyed and jobs exported, in which the public good and public infrastructure have been squandered. And they expressed outrage that the corporate elite, conservative politicians and pundits, and even other middle-class folk of the Tea-Party sort were now eager to not only cut the wages of public workers of every sort, but also savage democratic rights and the progressive services we have helped to create.

The democratic spirit and energy – that's what brought me to tears. Here in Madison, Wisconsin – here in the heart of the state – here in America's heartland – working people in all their diversity were once again coming together in solidarity. It has been in the making for thirty years and more. Sadly, it did not arise sooner. But that is history – a history not to forget and a history from which to learn – but, nonetheless, history. Now we have the making of a democratic surge. This is what democracy looks like, I thought. Liberty – Government – Legislation – Justice. *Forward!*

4

We Will Not Forget Wisconsin Workers' Struggles

On May 5, 1886, thousands of Milwaukee workers marched peacefully on the huge Bay View Rolling Mills as part of a nationwide effort to bring about the eight-hour day. On orders from Gov. Jeremiah Rusk, the state militia fired on the marchers, killing seven. The bloodiest labor disturbance in Wisconsin history, it began a new struggle for a more humane workplace and a more just society. On Sunday, May 1, 2011 – with our own Wisconsin Rising still in our hearts and minds – some 300 Wisconsinites gathered in solidarity at the state historical marker and monument to the tragedy in Bay View to commemorate the 125th anniversary of the tragedy. I delivered the following speech that afternoon on behalf of the Wisconsin Labor History Society.

Those who marched 125 years ago had left behind kings, aristocrats, landlords, and masters. And they had come to a nation of citizens, not subjects. A nation that declared: *All men are created equal...endowed by their Creator with certain unalienable rights... among these are life, liberty and the pursuit of happiness.* A nation in which "We the People" rule!

Truly, those who marched that day had joined a people who had fought a revolution – a revolution not only for independence, but also to make a Democratic republic; indeed, a people who had fought a Civil War – a Civil War not only to sustain the union, but also to assure that in it, freedom prevailed over slavery.

Life was challenging and demanding – to say the least. But the challenges and demands were no worse than those which they had known before. And in any case, those who marched

26

could see the possibilities here in the place that the revolutionary Thomas Paine had called an "Asylum for Mankind."

Moreover, they grasped America's purpose and promise and felt the nation's democratic imperative and impulse – perhaps more clearly and more dearly than those who had come to this place before them.

At the same time, they recognized that "*a new birth of freedom*" was never given – but had to be won. Those who marched had come a long way – and they had no intention of failing themselves, their families, their comrades, *or* their new home, America.

So, we gather here not simply to remember and honor them, but all the more to draw inspiration, strength and courage from their commitment, their determination, their hopes and their aspirations.

Many generations of working people have come to this town on the lakeshore with its diverse faiths and ethnicities – not to mention its love of beer, baseball, brats and babies. And together, here in Milwaukee and beyond, they created great things –the greatest city in Wisconsin, the greatest state in America, the greatest nation in history.

But of course, there are those who have denied and continue to deny America's purpose and promise. And they have fought us every step of the way.

You know who they are. They put power, property and profits over personhood. They insist that the American Dream is fulfilled. They proclaim that history ended in 1776 – or in 1848, or in 1865, or in 1920, or in 1945, or in 1965, or whenever.

But such folks don't get it….Better said, they get it, but they don't want us to get it!

They don't want us to remember what the likes of Thomas Paine, Frederick Douglass, Abraham Lincoln, Eugene Debs, Emma Goldman, Robert La Follette, Franklin and Eleanor Roosevelt, Martin Luther King Jr., César Chávez and those whose sacrifices we commemorate here today never forgot.

They don't want us to remember that we are descended from people who – for all their faults and failings – fought a revolution, a civil war, and a world war, not in hopes of defending the status quo, but in hopes of realizing freedom of speech...freedom of worship...freedom from want...freedom from fear...

They want us to forget that we are the children of people who built homes, livelihoods and communities, who organized political parties and labor unions and struggled for their rights as Americans – not just because they needed to, but also because they had made the Grand American Experiment of extending and deepening freedom, equality and democracy their own.

In fact, those who deny America's purpose and promise don't want us even to feel. They don't want us to feel America's democratic impulse – an impulse that not only led working men and women to come to Wisconsin; to build this community; to organize a union; and to dream of an Eight-Hour Day – eight hours for work, eight hours for rest, eight hours for what we will – but also led them to march here in Bay View on May 5, 1886.

But we will not stop remembering or feeling...

We will remember them, and we will honor them.

Against the ambitions and schemes of those who would deny America's purpose and promise: We will continue to gather in solidarity. We will continue to fight for our rights. And we will continue to declare that *"This is what democracy looks like!"*

Time to March on Washington Again for Jobs and Freedoms: An Open Letter to AFL-CIO President Richard Trumka

First posted at Salon, November 13, 2012.

Dear Brother Trumka -

Next year will mark the 50th anniversary of the March on Washington for Jobs and Freedom. Rallied by the great black union leader A. Philip Randolph, the president of the Brotherhood of Sleeping Car Porters, with the assistance of civil rights organizer Bayard Rustin and UAW president Walter Reuther, 250,000 Americans of every color and creed turned out on the National Mall on August 28, 1963 to demonstrate their support for guaranteeing equal rights and affording "life, liberty, and the pursuit of happiness" to all Americans. And it is a day that generations will forever remember because of the words spoken on the steps of the Lincoln Memorial by the Reverend Martin Luther King, Jr.: "I have a dream."

No doubt plans are already underway to commemorate that event. But we who believe in America's purpose and promise of extending and deepening freedom, equality, and democracy must do more than commemorate it. We must truly honor it. And to do that, we cannot wait until August.

Indeed, we need to not just recall but actually redeem the progressive spirit and vision of Randolph, Rustin, Reuther, and King. We need to march.

Randolph first developed the idea of a March on Washington in the spring of 1941. Inspired to act by President Franklin Roosevelt's State of the Union Address proclaiming the Four Freedoms – "Freedom of speech and expression, Freedom of worship, Freedom from want, Freedom from fear," – Randolph and his union brothers mobilized African Americans across the country to organize in favor of going to the nation's capital and demanding the opening up of America's expanding war industries to black workers.

It was a march that never took place. But the mobilization worked. The very prospect of an event that, as Randolph told FDR, promised to bring 100,000 blacks to a still-segregated Washington D.C., compelled the President – who, Randolph came to believe, actually welcomed the push – to bypass a Congress dominated by a conservative coalition of Republicans and southern Democrats and issue an executive order commanding the desegregation of the war plants.

Randolph, however, did not give up the idea of the March. And 22 years later, once again seeking to make a Democratic president do the right thing, he revived the March on Washington movement and this time, with an unprecedented grand coalition of rights, religious, and labor groups, staged the historic gathering.

Historians tell us that the March, while a magnificent event, did not work. That Kennedy hesitated and Congress delayed. But the scholars miss the point. The American people were moved and, though Kennedy was assassinated that November, his presidential successor Lyndon Johnson was even more determined to act. And empowered by courageous non-violent protestors, a generation of Americans who now recognized what America's promise demanded, a series of AFL-CIO lobbying campaigns, the new President and the civil rights movement secured the enactment of the Civil Rights Act, the Voting Rights Act, the Economic Opportunity Act, and the expansion of Social Security to include Medicare and Medicaid.

After more than thirty years of subordinating the public good to corporate priorities and private greed, of subjecting ourselves to widening inequality and intensifying insecurities, of allowing our industries and infrastructure to decay, of suffering culture wars and rightwing initiatives to roll back the rights that generations of Americans fought to secure – indeed, of denying our own democratic memories, impulses, and yearnings – we need to march.

Sadly, we need to march because we did not march before.

In 2008 we elected a President who reminded us all that "Yes, We Can." And in the face of the worst economic crisis since the Great Depression much was done. But as we well know, not enough. And because we left the public square vacant and public debate to be managed by cable tv hosts and inside-the-beltway pundits, a Tea Party movement emerged that propelled the GOP to huge victories in 2010 – victories that allowed the right and conservative rich to continue to pursue both culture wars and, yes, I will say it, class war from above. Indeed, they proceeded to not only block critical legislative initiatives in Washington, but also pass laws at the state level that abolished workers' rights, laid siege to women's rights, licensed the harassment of people of color, and made it difficult for too many folks to exercise the fundamental right of voting.

Brother Trumka, we need to stage a new March on Washington. Now especially, we need to march.

Voting last week, we expressed our determination to not only defend what our grandparents, parents, and we ourselves have accomplished, but the march of freedom. And yet, only days later we hear talk of "grand deals" in which House Republicans will agree on a way to raise taxes on the rich and the President and Democrats will make "necessary" cuts to "entitlements."

We need to march. As you said on November 8th: "Working people – union and non-union alike – say NO to cuts to Social Security, Medicare and Medicaid and YES to fair taxes on the wealthiest 2 percent."

But we need to march not just to say "No."

We need to march to strengthen the will of the President

31

and prevent him from once again deferring to congressional conservatives. We need to march to bolster our liberal and progressive representatives in their efforts to resist the pressure to compromise. And we need to march to encourage and mobilize our fellow citizens to not only demand what the majority of them voted for, but also to turn out in even greater numbers in 2014 to make sure we get it.

So, Brother Trumka, rally the union movement, gather up a new progressive coalition of rights, religious, and labor groups, of Americans in all their diversity, of Americans who want to not simply defend but democratically advance the promise of the Four Freedoms that inspired Randolph and the dream which sustained King. It is time to march.

6

The Struggle for Paine's Memory and American Democracy

Drawn from my book **Thomas Paine and the Promise of America** *(Hill & Wang, 2005), I presented this talk as the keynote address at a conference at the People's History Museum in Manchester, England in November 2013. The lecture was later published in Sam Edwards and Marcus Morris, eds.* **The Legacy of Thomas Paine in the Transatlantic World** *(Routledge, 2018).*

Thomas Paine has been my hero ever since I was a child – really, ever since I was a child, no more than 10 or 11 years old. And it's probably due to my grandfather – a New York City trial lawyer who grew up on New York's Lower East Side.

My grandparents eventually came to live in the Borough of Brooklyn right across the street from the Brooklyn Museum. And I loved to visit them...However, whenever they began to speak in Yiddish, I knew it was a signal for me to leave the room...

Now, if an older cousin were around, I would get him to take me over to the Museum to explore the galleries... But if no cousin were available, I would wander my grandparents' apartment as if it were a museum – each room a gallery.

And I always ended up at the far end of the dining room, where my grandfather kept a small collection of his personal books. I can still see those shelves. It was there, sitting on the floor, reaching for titles, that I first met Thomas Paine – originally by way of a book by the freethinker Joseph Lewis – a book in which he argued that it was Paine, not Jefferson, who had authored the Declaration of Independence...

Indeed, it was that book that instigated a rebellion on my part as I soon took to arguing with my teachers about who really authored the Declaration. And stubbornly, I always got the question wrong on exams.

In any case, I figured that if my learned grandfather thought so much of Paine, then I should too… In fact, when my grandmother passed away and my grandfather moved apartments, he gave me a few of his Paine books. I didn't get everything I read, but Paine became my hero – and however much other historical figures may have inspired my youthful political progressivism, Paine did so most of all.

As I saw it, historians needed to engage not only the historical past, but also historical memory, for as the American political scientist Wilson Carey McWilliams once wrote, "a people's memory sets the measure of its political freedom." And to make the long story short, I set out not only to debunk the arguments of the Right, but also to cultivate the memory of the American radical tradition – all of which led me back to Thomas Paine – and to the writing of a young adult biography.

Yet I still felt the need to do more – plus, I did not want to give up working on my boyhood hero so soon. I didn't feel we needed another full-scale treatment of his life, for we had two truly excellent adult biographies in those by John Keane and Jack Fruchtman, as well as Eric Foner's fabulous *Tom Paine and Revolutionary America*.

But I did feel Americans needed to hear more about Paine.

So I proposed a book of three parts: in Part One, I would recount Paine's life and labors; in Part Two I would relate the story of the suppression of his memory; and in Part Three, I would essentially resurrect Paine and have him speak to Americans today – which led a friend of mine, a Lutheran minister, to suggest that I follow the fashion of those young evangelicals who were wearing bracelets bearing the letters "WWJD" ("What Would Jesus Do?), and create a line of jewelry engraved with the letters "WWTPD."

But the new book turned into something else, something quite different than I had expected, for I discovered that I was very much mistaken – indeed, that we were all very much mistaken – about Paine's afterlife. No, I did not discover that the 19th Century American spiritualists who loved to "channel" Paine more than anybody else had been right all along. Rather, I kept encountering evidence that contradicted the long-told tale of Paine's exile from American public life. In fact, what I came across indicated that Americans had never forgotten Paine. Truly, never!

Yes, efforts continually were made to suppress appreciative remembrance of him. Yes, lies were told and crude things were propagated. And yes, he was both effectively banished from "official" memory and sadly despised in orthodox religious circles. However, I found that Paine actually had remained very much alive in American memory. More importantly, I found that he had remained very powerfully engaged in the making of American freedom, equality, and democracy – and I ended up telling a critically different story than I had projected.

So, this evening I speak to you of "The Struggle for Paine's Memory and the Making of American Democracy" – closing with some remarks on the amazing appropriation of Paine by the political right.

Ultimately, you will hear that the struggle for Paine's memory continues – but also that it has changed... And not necessarily for the better.

On July 17, 1980, Ronald Reagan stood before the Republican National Convention and the American people to accept his party's nomination for President of the United States. Most of what he said that evening was to be expected from a Republican. He spoke of the nation's past and its "shared values"; he attacked the incumbent Carter Administration and promised to lower taxes, limit government, and expand national defense; and he invited Americans to join him in a "crusade to make America great again."

Yet Reagan had much more than restoration in mind. He intended to transform American political life. He had constructed a new Republican alliance – a New Right – of corporate elites, Christian evangelicals, conservative intellectuals, and a host of right-wing interest groups in hopes of undoing the liberal achievements of the previous 40 years AND establishing a new national governing consensus.

All of that was well known. But that night Reagan startled many a listener – both Right and Left – by calling forth Thomas Paine and quoting his words from *Common Sense*: "We have it in our power to begin the world over again."

American politicians have always drawn upon the words and deeds of the Founders. Nevertheless, in quoting Paine, Reagan broke emphatically with longstanding conservative practice. Paine was not like George Washington, Benjamin Franklin, John Adams, Alexander Hamilton, and Thomas Jefferson. Paine had never really been admitted to the most select ranks of the Founding Fathers.

Recent presidents, mostly Democrats, had referred to him, but even the liberals had generally refrained from quoting Paine the revolutionary. They usually conjured up Paine the patriot, citing the line with which he opened the first of his American Crisis papers: "These are the times that try men's souls."

Conservatives certainly were not supposed to speak favorably of Paine – and for 200 years they had not. In fact, for generations they had publicly despised Paine and tried to bury his memory and legacy. And one can understand why. Endowing American experience with democratic impulse and aspiration, Paine had turned Americans into radicals and Americans have remained – I can feel the rising skepticism in the room – radicals at heart ever since.

Thomas Paine was the greatest radical of a radical age – we know that. Yet this son of an English artisan, who carried with him the idea of the Freeborn Briton, did not truly become a radical until his arrival in America in late 1774 at the age of 37. And even then, he apparently had never expected such things to happen. But struck by Americans' startling contradictions, energies, and possibilities, Paine dedicated himself to the American cause. Through his pamphleteering – and words such as "The sun never shined on a cause of greater worth" – Paine not only emboldened Americans to turn their colonial rebellion into a revolutionary war, but also inspired them to create a republic; defined the new nation in a democratically expansive and progressive fashion; and yes, articulated an American identity charged with historic purpose and promise.

Moreover, he served the cause as not only a pamphleteer, but also as a soldier, statesman, and donor. And at war's end, he was a popular hero.

Still, he was not finished. The story is told of a dinner gathering at which Paine, on hearing his mentor Benjamin Franklin observe, "Where liberty is, there is my country," cried out, "Where liberty is not, there is my country."

Truly, America's struggle had turned Paine into an inveterate champion of liberty, equality, and democracy, and after the war he went on to apply his pen to fresh struggles. In *Rights of Man,* he defended the French Revolution, challenged Britain's monarchical and aristocratic order, and outlined a series of public initiatives to improve the lives of working people. In *The Age of Reason,* he criticized organized religion, the claims of Biblical Scripture, and the power of churches and clerics. And in *Agrarian Justice,* he pioneered social democracy by proposing a means of addressing poverty that entailed taxing the landed rich to provide grants to the young and pensions for the elderly.

Reared an Englishman, adopted by America, and honored as a Frenchman, Paine often called himself a "citizen of the world." But the United States always remained paramount in his thoughts and evident in his labors.

And yet as great as his contributions were, they were not always appreciated, and his affections were not always reciprocated. His radical-democratic lines, style, and appeal – as well as his background, confidence, and single-mindedness – antagonized many among the powerful, propertied, prestigious, and pious and made him enemies even within the ranks of his fellow patriots. New England patricians and ministers, Middle Atlantic merchants and manufacturers, Southern slaveholders and preachers – feared the power of Paine's pen and the implications of his arguments. In reaction, they and their heirs sought to disparage his character, suppress his memory, and limit the influence of his ideas. And according to most accounts they succeeded.

For much of the nineteenth century, and well into the twentieth, Paine's pivotal role in the making of the United States was effectively erased in the official telling. Writing in the 1880s, future-President Theodore Roosevelt believed he could characterize Paine, with impunity, as a "filthy little atheist" (though Paine was neither filthy, little, nor an atheist).

Not only in the highest circles, but also in various popular quarters – particularly among the religiously devout – Paine's name conjured up the worst images, leading generations of historians and biographers to assume that memory of Paine's contributions to American history had been lost.

In the early 1940s, historian Dixon Wecter observed that, "To trace the curve of Paine's reputation is to learn something about hero-worship in reverse." And as recently as the 1990s, the chief scholar of the Founding, Gordon Wood, could state that Paine "seems destined to remain a misfit, an outsider."

Yet those accounts were wrong.

Paine had died, but neither his memory nor his legacy ever expired. His contributions were too fundamental and his vision of the nation too firmly imbued in the dynamic of American political life and culture to be so easily shed or suppressed.

Especially at times of crisis, when the nation's promise seemed truly in jeopardy – Americans, almost instinctively, would turn to Paine and his words. Even those who disdained him and what he represented could not fail to draw on his vision. Moreover, there were those who would not allow him and his arguments to be forgotten.

Contrary to the ambitions of the governing elites – to the presumptions of historians and biographers – Paine remained a powerful presence in American political and intellectual life. Recognizing the contradictions between the nation's ideals and reality, rebels, reformers, and critics – both native-born and immigrant – repeatedly recovered Paine's life and labors and drew ideas, inspiration, and encouragement from them as they struggled to defend, extend, and deepen freedom, equality, and democracy. Some honored Paine in memorials. Many more honored him all the more by adopting his arguments and words as their own.

Workingmen's advocates, freethinkers, abolitionists, suffragists, anarchists, populists, progressives, socialists, labor organizers, and liberals have repeatedly garnered political and intellectual energy from Paine, renewed his presence in American life, and served as the prophetic memory of his democratic vision of America.

The Painite roster is lengthy... So I will be very selective.

As we know, Paine had departed Philadelphia for Europe in 1787, hoping to secure funds to erect his projected iron bridge. Yet even in his absence he would remain a radical-democratic presence. Thrilling Jefferson and his allies, *Rights of Man* played a critical role in the emergence in the 1790s of both the Democratic-Republican Societies and the Republican Party. And those same texts not only inspired many an English, Scottish, Welsh, and

Irish radical, but also, when royal repression ensued, to seek refuge in Paine's proclaimed "asylum for mankind," where they continued to serve the cause of republican democracy as periodical editors and writers.

Moreover, Paine's literary assault on organized religion fomented a short-lived, but vibrant Deist movement that – from Cambridge, Mass to the Carolinas – included both working people and college students.

Yet there's more. Undeniably, *The Age of Reason* shocked the Christian faithful. Nevertheless, many an evangelical – from the Baptist revivalist John Leland to the peripatetic Methodist preacher Lorenzo Dow – continued to draw upon Paine and his arguments as they challenged Church Establishments and clerical power structures.

For all of his nasty ranting, John Adams was quite perceptive and prescient about modern history when he wrote:

> I know not whether any man in the world has had more influence on its inhabitants or affairs for the last thirty years than Tom Paine... For such a mongrel between pigs and puppy, begotten by a wild boar on a bitch wolf, never before in any age of the world was suffered by the poltroonery of mankind to run through such a career of mischief. Call it then the Age of Paine.

Eager to limit the power of the people, the powers that be did their best to squelch remembrance of democracy's great champion. But just as Paine had expected, they would not easily fall into line. They would make the first half of the nineteenth century not only a time of "Manifest Destiny," but also a time of "militant democracy." And they would affectionately carry Paine with them as they did.

Intent on embalming the Revolution more than celebrating it, orators at official Independence Day commemorations glorified

Washington and – depending on the state wherein they spoke – Adams, Hamilton, Franklin, or Jefferson. But those who wielded power and purse did not want to hear of Paine, and they figured others should not either, at least not in any appreciative way. Nevertheless, from the towns and cities of the East to those of what we now call the Midwest, radicals and liberals – again, both immigrant and native – staged their own commemorative events. Gathered together, they joyously recalled Paine and his words to redeem America's revolutionary heritage and, therewith, empower workingmen, create egalitarian communities, secure the separation of church and state, speak freely, and revere the creation free-mindedly.

Still others turned to Paine as they pursued the liberation of black Americans from bondage and the establishment of women's equal rights as citizens. Utopians and freethinkers like Robert Owen and Fanny Wright, "Workies" like William Heighton, Thomas Skidmore, and George Henry Evans, abolitionists like William Lloyd Garrison and Wendell Phillips, suffragists like Elizabeth Cady Stanton, Ernestine Rose, and Susan B. Anthony, along with armies of others, read Paine, recited his words, and spurred themselves and their comrades into action.

Paine also fired the imaginations both of Spiritualists – most of whom were rather progressive on matters of class, race, and gender – and of Transcendentalists. Ralph Waldo Emerson would write that, "Each man...is a tyrant in tendency, because he would impose his ideas on others. Jesus would absorb the race; but Tom Paine...helps humanity by resisting this exuberance of power."

Concurrently, the early Young American movement – a cohort of New York political and literary figures associated with the Democratic Party – embraced Paine's progressive and expansionary vision of America's future *and* cultivated his memory in its magazine, *The United States and Democratic Review*. Admittedly, some would turn into pro-imperialists and even worse. But the movement shaped the thinking of two of America's greatest democratic writers, novelist Herman Melville and poet and essayist Walt Whitman, who, as their works attest, remained Painites for their entire lives. Forever hoping Americans would absorb him as affectionately as he had absorbed them, Whitman wanted not simply to "help set the memory of Paine right," but also to become the new Thomas Paine. And while Whitman did not know it, Abraham Lincoln – his poetic "Captain" of *Leaves of Grass* – had absorbed Paine, as well.

We now acknowledge the young Abe as a Deist. But he apparently learned more than skepticism from Paine. Roy Basler, the editor of Lincoln's *Collected Works*, noted that Paine was probably Lincoln's "favorite author," from whom the future President received his "most important literary education" and in whose writings he found his "model of eloquence." And if we listen carefully, we can definitely hear Paine's words regarding freedom and America's extraordinary purpose and promise echoing through Lincoln's finest speeches.

Examples abound of those who turned to Paine – increasingly so as civil war threatened. But here I'll simply cite the testimony of the Unitarian minister and abolitionist Moncure Conway. In an 1860 Paine birthday address in Cincinnati, Conway observed that, "Thomas Paine's life up to 1809…is interesting; but Thomas Paine's life from that time to [now] is more than interesting – it is thrilling!"

And Conway's observation would aptly describe the later decades of the century as well… Experiencing explosive growth and development, Gilded Age America witnessed new forms of exploitation and widening inequalities. But as much as the governing classes might have wished it otherwise, they confronted vigorous struggles to extend and deepen freedom, equality, and democracy – AND, just as their predecessors had, the new generations of radicals and reformers would find ideas, inspiration, and encouragement in Paine.

A host of intellectuals honored Paine's life and memory. Republican lawyer Robert Ingersoll – the foremost lecturer of his day and the leading advocate of religious skepticism – so admired Paine that he defended and promoted him everywhere he went. The father of American sociology, Lester Ward, challenged the Social Darwinism of Herbert Spencer and William Graham Sumner with Painite ideas about freedom and human possibilities. And after reading Paine's work on the Mississippi, Mark Twain, America's greatest storyteller, was so convinced that Paine was one of the most important men in history that he proceeded to incorporate his democratic arguments into his fiction and commentaries, most evidently so in *A Connecticut Yankee in King Arthur's Court*.

Even as Teddy Roosevelt was scribbling paeans to the rich merchant Founder Gouvernor Morris and stupidities about Paine, smarter scholars were recovering and recounting his contributions. Cornell professor Moses Coit Tyler delivered a talk on Paine at the very first American Historical Association conference in 1884 and devoted entire chapters to Paine in his pioneering *Literary History of the American Revolution*. And that same year, Moncure Conway became the first president of the Thomas Paine National Historical Association and then went on to publish a magnificent two-volume biography of Paine and a four-volume collection of his writings.

Yet far more than the literati attended to Paine. Confronting the Robber Barons and their ilk, labor leaders like William Sylvis of the 1860s National Labor Union, Thomas Phillips of the 1880s Knights of Labor, and Eugene Debs of the 1890s American Railway Union found strength and direction in Paine's life and labors.

Paine continued to empower immigrants. In the wake of the 1848 Revolutions, cohorts of liberal and radical German refugees, like their British and Irish predecessors, came to Paine's "asylum for mankind" prepared to carry on the fight for a good society.

And fight they did. Joining with native-born labor unionists and social democrats, they and those who followed them to America actively served in the campaign for the eight-hour day and a democratic America. And they never forgot their hero. Every January 29, German-American workers, farmers, and intellectuals from New York to Milwaukee and from rural Wisconsin to the Texas Hill Country celebrated Paine's birthday with drinks, dining, and dancing.

Having studied Paine's works, Chicago's Haymarket Martyrs – as well as later anarchists such as the renowned Emma Goldman – clearly saw themselves advancing America's Revolutionary tradition.

Populists, Progressives, Suffragists, and Socialists – all, to varying degrees, admired Paine and joined him to their movements.

Plains-state and Southwestern politicians such as Kansas Congressman Jeremiah Simpson and Texan Judge Thomas Nugent appealed to farmers, miners, and other laboring folk with words straight out of Paine's *Rights of Man*.

Crusaders such as the attorney, editor, and advocate of labor and racial equality Louis Freeland Post and the muckraking journalist George Creel were motivated by Paine's career and ideas.

Feminists, from the radical Victoria Woodhull in the 1870s to the reformer Dr. Mary Putnam-Jacobi in the 1890s, quoted Paine at length on equality as they demanded the liberation and enfranchisement of their sex. And more than any on the left, Socialists – most notably, Julius Wayland, the publisher of the popular paper, *The Appeal to Reason*; Clarence Darrow, the renowned "Attorney for the Damned"; and Eugene Debs, now the Party leader and perennial presidential candidate – promoted Paine's democratic memory as they campaigned for a "cooperative commonwealth."

No less so, twentieth-century radicals and liberals would also reach back and grab hold of Paine – though, sadly, they would hardly do so in unison.

In fact, all too often they would do so in conflict with each other, as in 1917-1918, when the Wilson Administration – even as it was suppressing antiwar dissent and jailing many a Paine-inspired radical for sedition – was enlisting Paine's words in support of a war intended to make the world safe for democracy, and the President himself was deriving critical elements of his famous Fourteen Points from Paine's internationalist republican vision.

Still, for all of their efforts, pro-war liberals would not easily monopolize Paine. Arrested for sedition, Eugene Debs eloquently testified to a patriotism alternative to, if not grander than that of the Wilsonians by summoning a host of great American radicals to stand alongside him in the courtroom at his trial in Canton, Ohio – Paine positioned in front of all the rest.

Though capitalism, conservatism, racism, and anti-Semitism dominated 1920s America, progressive-minded scholars and public intellectuals such as William Dodd, Vernon Parrington, and Gilbert Seldes – not to mention infamous debunkers like H.L. Mencken and William Woodward in their own sly way – celebrated Paine as a means of challenging the capitalist and reactionary tenor of the times.

And in the 1930s – responding to both Great Depression crises and New Deal possibilities – leftwing writers, artists, and composers working on the "Cultural Front" made Paine a popular literary, visual, and lyrical reference as they advanced the cause of labor and pressed for further progressive initiatives.

But here I must tell you the story of a group of Bonus Marchers: In 1932, twenty thousand Great War veterans descended peacefully on Washington D.C. demanding that Congress and the Republican Administration give them the Veterans Bonus it had promised in 1924 to pay them in 1945. However, they were driven from the city by armed federal troops led by General

Douglas MacArthur.

Notably, one contingent of veterans headed north to New York City. And remarkably, they had not given up on America's promise. There, on the Hudson River shoreline, they set up a multiracial and cooperative "Hooverville" (as Depression-era shack towns were popularly dubbed). And they not only flew the "Stars and Stripes" over nearly every hut. They also named the place "Camp Thomas Paine."

No less notable: In 1940, First Lady Eleanor Roosevelt published *The Moral Basis of Democracy* – a book in which she challenged her fellow citizens to respond to the rise of fascism overseas by renewing the struggle for freedom and equality in America. And she devoted far more of her pages to Thomas Paine and his democratic arguments than to any other figure.

Moreover, the passion for Paine would continue to grow as Americans anxiously witnessed the conquest of Europe and East Asia by Hitler and the Japanese Imperialists, respectively, and then – as much as they hoped otherwise – had to deal with them head-on in the wake of the attack on Pearl Harbor.

Dramatically attesting to Americans' persistent affection for Paine, President Franklin Delano Roosevelt himself urgently called him back to military service in a Washington's Birthday "fireside chat" of February 23, 1942 – a speech considered one of Roosevelt's best ever. Confronting the nation's most severe crisis since the Civil War, FDR made clear the demands of global warfare, laid out a vision of a world shaped by the Four Freedoms – "Freedom of Speech, Freedom of Worship, Freedom from Want, and Freedom from Fear" – and called upon his fellow citizens to work hard and fight energetically in pursuit of victory and peace. Finally – knowing that he had to inspire and encourage his fellow citizens, not antagonize or alienate them – the President concluded with:

"These are the times that try men's souls." Tom Paine wrote

those words on a drumhead, by the light of a campfire. That was when Washington's little army of ragged, rugged men was retreating across New Jersey, having tasted naught but defeat. And General Washington ordered that these great words written by Tom Paine be read to the men of every regiment in the Continental Army, and this was the assurance given to the first American armed forces: "The summer soldier and the sunshine patriot will, in this crisis, shrink from the service of their country; but he that stands it now, deserves the love and thanks of man and woman. Tyranny, like hell, is not easily conquered; yet we have this consolation with us, that the harder the sacrifice, the more glorious the triumph." So spoke Americans in the year 1776. So speak Americans today!

And Americans not only responded as never before – taking Paine with them into every front of the war. They named a Liberty Ship and a B-17 Flying Fortress after him. They produced radio programs about him. And they published new Paine biographies, Paine anthologies, and even Paine comic books for kids. In fact, they turned Howard Fast's 1943 novel, *Citizen Tom Paine*, into a bestseller.

I could go on to relate the continuing progressive presence of Paine through the 1950s Cold War, the Sixties movements and upheavals, and the 1970s Conservative ascendance. But I'll move directly to Paine today...

Heartened and animated by Paine, Americans have pressed for the rights of workingmen; insisted upon freedom of conscience and the separation of church and state; demanded the abolition of slavery; campaigned for the equality of women; confronted the power of property and wealth; opposed the tyrannies of Fascism and Communism; fought a second Revolution for racial justice and equality; and challenged our own government's authorities and policies, domestic and foreign.

Yes, defeats were suffered, mistakes were committed, and tragic and ironic turnabouts were endured. But great victories were achieved. And now, it actually looks like we have all become Painites.

Today, references to Paine abound in public debate and culture; and in contrast to the past, not only the left, but also, in the wake of Reagan, the right claims him as one of their own – leading Paine biographer Jack Fruchtman to muse, "Who owns Tom Paine?" Paine has definitely achieved a new status in public history and memory. The very extent of it has made it seem as if it had never been otherwise.

Reporting on a campaign to have a marble statue of suffragists Susan B. Anthony, Elizabeth Cady Stanton, and Lucretia Mott moved into the capitol Rotunda, a Washington-based journalist wrote, "Imagine a statue of Benjamin Franklin shoved into a broom closet in the White House. Or a portrait of Thomas Paine tucked behind a door. That would never happen." While I love the sentiment, I wonder about the amnesia it suggests.

In any case, the battle is no longer over the question of whether we will publicly remember Paine, but what we will remember him for. And it remains critical to the struggle for American democracy.

Historically, Americans have turned to their Revolutionary past – and to Thomas Paine in particular – at times of national crisis, when, as I have said, the very purpose and promise of America seemed at risk or in doubt. And today, Americans once again confront major questions and crises: globalization, terrorism international and domestic, intensifying class inequalities, fiscal disasters, joblessness, and declining opportunities.

Like other generations before ours, we Americans look back to those who themselves faced and overcame such crises for answers, inspiration, and encouragement. And we do battle over the meaning of America – over the meaning of its purpose and promise.

You may scoff at the idea of "America's purpose and promise." Left academics and pundits back home do so regularly. But they blunder in doing so. It is not a one-dimensional idea. Democratically articulated – starting with Paine – it empowered generations of democratic activism and, for all the tragedy and irony that has marked American history, actions in pursuit of that promise have liberated millions. All of which American right-wingers know all too well. Which is why they now so ardently seek to lay claim to Paine – or better said, to hijack him to their cause.

Not all of him, of course. Just some of his lines. And licensed by Reagan, they all do it. But whereas Reagan – who was a Roosevelt New-Deal Democrat in the 1930s and 40s – caught us by surprise and recited "We have it in our power to begin the world over again," his rightwing heirs – whatever else they also rip off – usually go straight to Paine's line in *Common Sense*: "Society in every state is a blessing, but government, even in its best state, is but a necessary evil."

Indeed, from rightwing heartthrob Sarah Palin to the cutely costumed Tea Partiers, that one has become their mantra. In 2009, the 200th anniversary of Paine's passing, Glenn Beck, a rightwing talking-head – then at the peak of his powers and public presence – released *Glenn Beck's Common Sense: The Case Against an Out-of-Control Government, Inspired by Thomas Paine.* And no joke, describing Thomas Paine as the "Glenn Beck of the American Revolution," Beck went on the road to promote it and succeeded in turning it into a national bestseller. And I am sure you will not be surprised to hear that nearly every one of Beck's so-called *Common Sense* arguments perversely warped, contradicted, or trashed those of Paine.

I was not terribly surprised by the effort or the heat generated. But I was sadly disappointed by the response of many a liberal and leftist. Oh yes, some progressive pundits challenged Beck's assertions. But liberal politicians and pundits did not seek to reclaim Paine, articulate a radical-democratic vision of America, and try to remind Americans of who they were and might yet accomplish.

Of course, I should have expected it. The Democrats are no less culpable for the Conservative Ascendance of the past 40 years than the Republicans. And while the majority of Americans registered their persistent democratic hopes and aspirations by electing Barack Obama as President, he signaled his own moderation, if not presidential deference, in his January 2009 Inaugural Address. I could point to many things. But most telling, perhaps, is that even as he recited words from Paine's first Crisis – which startled me – Obama never mentioned Paine's name.

And that spring – even as the Tea Party both recruited hordes of angry middle-class white guys to occupy public squares and garnered dollars aplenty from the rightwing rich to flood the airwaves with ads – the new President and his party made no effort to mobilize Americans to pursue their campaign promises of taxing the wealthy, empowering workers, restoring the wall separating church and state, and enacting a truly democratic national healthcare plan.

Before I really start to rant, I will close by saying that American liberals, progressives, and radicals need to do what generations of their predecessors did: Read Paine. Think grandly. Articulate America's promise anew. And have enough faith in their fellow citizens to engage them not simply as cable-television consumers, but all the more as citizens who are capable of redeeming the promise and renewing the struggle for freedom, equality, and democracy.

7

Remember and Honor FDR Progressively
– *"Make America Fairly Radical for a Generation"*

Drawn in good part from my work on **The Fight for the Four Freedoms: What Made FDR and the Greatest Generation Truly Great** *(Simon & Schuster, 2014), this speech was first delivered at the Franklin D. Roosevelt Four Freedoms Park on Roosevelt Island in New York City on April 12, 2014 and then at the FDR Library and Home in Hyde Park, New York on June 21, 2014.*

When I began work on *The Fight for the Four Freedoms: What Made FDR and the Greatest Generation Truly Great,* I had the good fortune of coming upon the depression-era and wartime essays of the progressive columnist Max Lerner: I not only liked what I read... It often seemed as though he was saying exactly what I would have said at that time. I especially appreciated what he had to say about American history.

In a book published on the very eve of World War II – a work he brilliantly titled *It Is Later Than You Think: The Need for a Militant Democracy* – Lerner wrote: "The basic story in the American past, the only story ultimately worth the telling, is the story of the struggle between the creative and the frustrating elements in the democratic adventure."

I now put that proposition at the top of all of my course syllabi – and I am sure that if President Roosevelt happened to read those words he too must have relished them, for he continually advanced that very story of America in all of his greatest speeches.

Lerner himself stood to the left of Roosevelt. But in critical ways he stood firmly with the President. And when I thought about what I would say this afternoon, I could not help but recall the column "FDR: The People Remember" – which Lerner published 68 years ago, in 1946, on the first anniversary of FDR's passing. In that column, Lerner wrote: "A few days ago, when it had become clear that the whole nation would observe the first anniversary of FDR's death... the *New York Daily News* [which had always hated FDR] published a griping editorial. Why, it asked, should Americans be observing both Roosevelt's birthday and his death-day? Even for Washington and Lincoln one observance day was enough. Why should this fellow rate two?"

"The answer," Lerner replied, "is that the people remember in their own way." And recalling how Roosevelt had rallied Americans to fight first the Great Depression and then Fascism – Lerner spoke of how they might well be remembering their late President:

> They remember the collapse of an economy in 1929, the pathetic inaction of the men who boasted themselves the leaders of America, the Hoovervilles, the bread lines, the farmers' riots, the bonus march, the battle of Anacostia Flats, the blank and fearful despair of the world's greatest nation...
>
> They remember the crippled man to whom they turned for leadership... They remember his words: *'The only thing we have to fear is fear itself,'* and the succession of crisis measures that came with the staccato authority of communiqués from a battlefield. They remember the hope that began surging back into their hearts, the sense that whatever mistakes might be made, America had found its greatness again."

And Lerner spoke in equally moving terms of how they were probably recalling FDR's wartime leadership: "They remember the looming shadow of fascist power; the man who recognized the enemy for what it was, and sought against heartbreaking odds to educate a whole people out of their dream of peace and security to the awareness of danger... They remember the news of Pearl Harbor, the nation that overnight found itself knit together... the civilian who was their Commander-in-Chief and picked the generals who held in their hands the destinies of all the young Americans... They remember the day when the Continental wall was breached, and we knew victory would be ours...And they remember the spring day when the news came that he would no longer be with them to lead their victories and shoulder part of their burdens..."

I cite Lerner's column not to validate our own diverse efforts at remembering both Franklin Roosevelt's birth on January 30 and his passing on April 12 – but rather, because of the question it poses to us: *To us,* who were not there in the 1930s and 1940s – *To us,* who neither elected FDR to be President four times, nor served as "Soil Soldiers" in the CCC, GIs in the military, Rosie the Riveters in a war plant, or volunteers with the Red Cross or USO – *To us,* who have only heard the stories, read the books, and seen the movies.

That question is: "How and what do we remember of FDR?"

And for that matter: "How and what do we remember of the men and women whom we have come to call the Greatest Generation?"

Those of us who live in the long, long shadow of that President, of that generation, of all that they accomplished: How and what do we remember?

It is a critical question, for as the political scientist Wilson Carey McWilliams once observed: "A people's memory sets the measure of its political freedom."

Clearly, we do not fail to remember:

We have erected two magnificent FDR memorials – one in Washington D.C. and another here on Roosevelt Island. And we have built a great monument on the National Mall to those who fought World War II.

And yet, for all of the memorials, books, films, and public displays and gatherings, we are failing to remember the most significant thing – arguably, the most democratic and inspiring thing – the very thing that we now most need to remember.

Now, when all that they fought for is under siege and we, too, find ourselves confronting forces that threaten the nation and all that it stands for: *We are failing to remember What Made FDR and the Greatest Generation Truly Great.*

Yes, we remember that they rescued the United States from economic destruction in the Great Depression and defended it against fascism in the Second World War. *And yes,* we remember that they went on to turn the nation into the strongest and most prosperous country on earth.

However, at the cost of not only their memory and legacy, but also our own shared prospects and possibilities, we are failing to remember that they did all of that – against fierce antidemocratic opposition and despite their own terrible faults and failings – *by making America freer, more equal, and more democratic than ever before in the process.*

Indeed, we are forgetting what they themselves came to see all the more clearly in the course of saving the nation from economic ruin and political oblivion: *That the only way to truly defend, secure, and sustain American democratic life is to progressively enhance it.* I will say that again: *They came to see all the more clearly that the only way to truly defend, secure, and sustain American democratic life is to progressively enhance it.*

Franklin Roosevelt – who knew American history, who believed in America's historic purpose and promise, *and* who had extraordinary confidence in his fellow citizens – had come to know that truth even before they elected him their President. And he firmly believed that they knew it too.

In fact, he had learned about it not just from his reading of US history, but also from his fellow Americans, especially – with

Eleanor's assistance – from working people, men and women, rural and urban, immigrant and native-born.

It was that knowledge, that belief, and that confidence, which gave him the strength and courage, in the face of the worst economic and social catastrophe in American history, to state in 1930 that "There is no question in my mind that it is time for the country to become fairly radical for a generation"; to call in the 1932 presidential campaign for not only a New Deal, but also a "new economic declaration of rights"; and to declare in 1935 that: "Democracy is not a static thing... It is an everlasting march."

Moreover, Roosevelt was right: His fellow Americans did recognize it too – and they responded to his words and initiatives with energy, enthusiasm, and determination. Together, President and People severely tested each other, made terrible mistakes and regrettable compromises, and suffered tragic defeats and disappointments.

However, challenging each other to live up to their finest ideals and aspirations, they advanced them further than either had expected or even imagined possible.

They not only rejected authoritarianism. They also redeemed the nation's promise by initiating revolutionary changes in American government and public life and radically extending American freedom, equality, and democracy.

Through a host of alphabet-soup agencies and associations – from the SEC, the CCC, and the WPA, to the CIO, the AYC, and the NAACP – they subjected big business and banking to public account and regulation; they empowered government to address the needs of working people and they established a social security system; they organized labor unions, consumer campaigns, and civil-rights groups and they fought for their rights and broadened and leveled the "We" in "We the People"; they built schools, post offices, and parks; they expanded the public infrastructure with new roads, bridges, and dams; and they improved the American landscape and environment; *and* they cultivated the arts and refashioned popular culture – just think Swing Music. And in so doing, they imbued themselves with fresh democratic convictions, hopes, and aspirations.

All of which propelled the President – even as the Great Depression continued to haunt the nation and the armies of Nazi Germany and Imperial Japan were threatening to overrun the world east and west – to not only profess that "I do not look upon these United States as a finished product. We are still in the making"; to not only declare that "A true patriotism urges us to build an even more substantial America where the good things of life may be shared by more of us, where the social injustices will not be encouraged to flourish"; and to not only proclaim that "This generation has a rendezvous with destiny"; but also to articulate Americans' grandest strivings past and present in a promise of four fundamental freedoms.

In his 1941 State of the Union Message – after first rallying Americans to turn the United States into the "Arsenal of Democracy" and making it very clear that the defense of the nation called not for giving up what they had struggled so hard to achieve, but for strengthening "democratic life in America" by building upon those achievements – Roosevelt said: "In the future days, which we seek to make secure, we look forward to a world founded upon four essential human freedoms: first is freedom of speech and expression... The second is freedom of every person to worship God in his own way... The third is freedom from want... The fourth is freedom from fear..."

The vision was international. But Roosevelt rooted it firmly in American experience and aspiration. As he explained: "Since the beginning of our American history, we have been engaged in change – in a perpetual, peaceful revolution – a revolution which goes on steadily, quietly, adjusting itself to changing conditions without the concentration camp or the quicklime in the ditch. The world order which we seek is the cooperation of

free countries, working together in a friendly, civilized society."
And, as ever, Americans did not fail him or themselves.

In the name of the "Four Freedoms," 16,000,000 Americans were to put on uniforms and pursue a global struggle we would come to call the "Good War" – not for the character of the combat, but for the rightness of the cause and the unity of purpose in which the nation pursued it. With their allies, they would storm beaches, slog through jungles, tramp across icy fields, sail through submarine-infested waters, fly missions over heavily fortified territories, and punch, push, claw, and ultimately power their way to victory. And at the same time, their fellow Americans would not only pray for their safe return, but also – in their tens of millions – go "All Out!" both to provide the arms and materiel required for victory *and* to protect and improve what they were defending.

Once again, President and People were to test each other, make sorry mistakes and compromises, and suffer serious defeats and disappointments.

Yes, racism sorely marked the war effort: a racism that produced a Jim-Crow segregated military; a racism that interned Japanese Americans; a racism that instigated deadly urban riots.

Nevertheless, believing in the nation's historic purpose and promise – and refusing to be defined by that racism – American people of color would serve heroically in every phase of the war effort. And in all their diversity, Americans not only prevailed over their enemies, but also once again compelled each other to progressively enhance American democratic life in the process.

Conservatives and reactionaries did their damnedest to deny the promise of the Four Freedoms – even to the point of trying to deny overseas GIs the right to vote!

But despite that opposition, President and People expanded the labor, consumer, and civil-rights movements; subjected industry and the marketplace to greater public control; reduced inequality and poverty; and further transformed the meaning of the "We" in "We the People."

Moreover, they looked forward to pursuing new liberal and social-democratic initiatives at war's end: 83 percent of Americans wanted to expand Social Security to include national healthcare; 90 percent favored joint planning by "government, business, and labor... to do away with unemployment after the war;" and 73 percent supported not only launching New-Deal-style public-works projects to provide jobs after the war, but also a policy in which the federal government would actually "guarantee" a job to those needing one.

Empowered by those hopes and aspirations, the President – the same man who had called for a new "economic declaration of rights" in 1932 – now proceeded to propose in his 1944 State of the Union Address that the nation enact not only a GI Bill of Rights for the homecoming veterans, but also a Second Bill of Rights – *an Economic Bill of Rights for all Americans* – to make the promise of the Four Freedoms all the more real.

As he presented it, this Second Bill of Rights would include the right to a job with a living wage; the right of every family to a decent home; the right to healthcare; the right to security in old age; *and* the right to a good education.

But it was not to happen – for as much as an overwhelming majority of Americans wanted it, a right-wing congressional coalition opposed it.

And yet that coalition could not block the enactment of the famous GI Bill – a massive social-democratic program that was to enable 12,000,000 veterans, nearly 1 in 10 Americans, to progressively transform themselves and their country for the better.

President Roosevelt passed away in 1945. Nazi Germany and Imperial Japan surrendered in the months that followed. But the promise of the Four Freedoms did not expire. Even as the United States began to "take off" in an unprecedented economic expansion and enter into a "Cold War" struggle with the Soviet Union, most Americans set out to make that promise all the more real.

But not everyone... Conservatives, reactionaries, and corporate executives had their own ambitions for postwar America – and they spared no expense in trying to secure them.

Still, for all of their efforts and expenditures, they could not get Americans to forget or forsake their hard-won victories or the promise that encouraged them. In fact, as Americans continued to make their nation ever stronger and more prosperous, they also pushed freedom, equality, and democracy forward. Never as quickly or as completely as some wished; but always forward.

Picking up where they had left off in 1941, they built new communities, churches, schools, and civic associations; secured even higher living standards for themselves and their families; and – when they were seriously challenged in the 1960s to live up to the promise that so many of them had struggled to articulate and advance – they recommitted the nation to doing so.

The power of Roosevelt's Four Freedoms endured: Those who marched for civil rights, campaigned to end poverty, organized public employee unions, pushed to enact healthcare for the elderly and poor, demanded equal rights for women, reformed the nation's immigration law, expanded public education and the arts, pressed for regulating business and industry to protect the environment, workers, and consumers, and protested the Vietnam War did not regularly recite those freedoms. But there were quite a few who did. And they were not only inspired and informed by the struggles and achievements of the President and the People who first proclaimed and fought for those Four Freedoms.

They were also called to act anew by military and civilian veterans of that fight in the 1930s and 1940s – by figures whose names include not only Presidents John Kennedy and Lyndon Johnson, but also labor leaders, civil rights activists, feminists, and environmentalists such as A. Philip Randolph, Walter Reuther, Jerry Wurf, Cesar Chavez, Ella Baker, James Farmer, Betty Friedan, Rachel Carson, and Barry Commoner.

Undeniably, after more than thirty years of subordinating the public good to corporate priorities and private greed, after more than thirty years of subjecting ourselves to widening inequality and intensifying insecurities, after more than thirty years of denying our own democratic impulses and yearnings, and now especially, when our democratic rights are under renewed and continuous assault, the "Age of Roosevelt" and the progressive pursuit of the Four Freedoms can seem a very long time ago.

But ask yourselves:

Do we not embrace the promise of the Four Freedoms? Do we not feel the democratic impulse that our parents and grandparents passed on to us? And do we not yearn to enable America to "find its 'greatness' again"?

Of course we do. And yet, we seem to have forgotten how to do it.

So, we need to remember:

We need to remember who we are.

We need to remember that we are the children and grandchildren of the men and women who – inspired and encouraged by Franklin Delano Roosevelt – not only rescued the United States from economic destruction in the Great Depression, defended it against Fascism and Imperialism in the Second World War, and turned it into the strongest and most prosperous country in human history, but also did all of that by harnessing the powers of democratic government and making America freer, more equal, and more democratic than ever before.

We need to do more than remember, however. And here I turn again to Max Lerner: In July 1948 – just two years and a bit after he penned "FDR: The People Remember" – Lerner wrote a column he titled "The Waste of History."

With the memory of the previous 15 years still powerfully fresh and impressive – but now worried about not just the rightwing political reaction we would come to call McCarthyism, but also the failure of liberals and progressives to deal with it – Lerner said: "The creative capacity itself seems to have gone out of American political life." Lerner was not about to give up his democratic hopes, for as he observed: "What we did once we can resume." But he seriously lamented what he saw happening. "The tragedy," he observed, "lies in the waste of our experience, in the waiting while all the old blunders are committed over again."

Happily, it would turn out that our parents and grandparents were not about to waste their history. Sadly, however, it looks like we are doing just that.

So, we need not simply to remember. We need to do what President Roosevelt and our parents and grandparents did to defend, sustain, and secure American democratic life. *We need to enhance it.*

Or as FDR put it back in 1930: We need to make America "fairly radical for a generation."

8

David Brooks Asks "What is America For?" We Must Provide the Answer

Published at Moyers and Company, June 29, 2014

In his *New York Times* column of Friday, June 27, 2014, "The Spiritual Recession" conservative David Brooks posed the same question – "What is the country for?" – which he essentially first posed seventeen years ago in "A Return to National Greatness: A Manifesto for a Lost Creed" (*Weekly Standard*, March 3, 1997). And yet, no more than he did in 1997 does Brooks effectively answer that question today.

But, of course, as a conservative he cannot.

How could he possibly appreciate and write informatively of America's purpose and promise – the promise inscribed in our historical memory and imagination by Paine's *Common Sense*, Jefferson's Declaration, the Founders' Preamble to the Constitution and Bill of Rights, Lincoln's Gettysburg Address, FDR's Four Freedoms, and King's "I Have a Dream" speech?

How could he appreciate the promise that inspired not just a revolutionary war but also generations of Americans to struggle to expand both the "We" in "We the People" and the democratic process through which "the people" can genuinely govern themselves?

Nevertheless, that does not mean we can simply dismiss Brooks's question.

Then a writer and editor at Bill Kristol's *Weekly Standard*, Brooks wrote "A Return to National Greatness" because he believed America's governing class had dangerously abandoned the idea that America possessed world-historic purpose and promise – dangerous, Brooks explained, quoting Tocqueville, because "Democracy has a tendency to slide into nihilistic mediocrity if its citizens are not inspired by some larger national goal."

Brooks opened the essay by celebrating the ruling class of the late 19th-century Gilded Age for its commitment to the idea that "America's mission was to advance civilization itself." He then proceeded, no doubt to the chagrin of his political and intellectual comrades, to actually praise mid-20th-century liberals for their own sense of America's historical purpose and promise and their determination to "accomplish some great national endeavor" such as "Wilson's Fourteen Points, the New Deal, John F. Kennedy's New Frontier." Finally, after lambasting liberals for deferring to the New Left and embracing both "radical egalitarianism" and the notion that the "personal" was "political," Brooks turned his attentions to the right, not to applaud his comrades' vision of nation greatness, but to arraign them for having none.

As Brooks saw it, his fellow right-wingers were giving up the idea that the United States was endowed with special purpose and promise and essentially disabling themselves and the nation by pressing for "localism" over "federalism" and enthusiastically embracing "populism" versus "elitism" – to the point of leaving no opening for national projects and no room for leadership, in Jefferson's words, by a "natural aristocracy."

But Brooks wrote not merely to chastise. He did so to urge conservatives to think again, to change their course, and to develop a national project. He had no particular project in mind. In fact, he wrote: "It almost doesn't matter what great task government sets for itself, as long as it does some tangible thing with energy and effectiveness." In short: Just do it.

It is easy to criticize Brooks's call for "A Return to National Greatness." For example, his praise for America's Gilded Age ruling classes obscures the brutality of their rule. And while he does not hesitate to cite Democrats Wilson and Kennedy, he seems incapable of mentioning Franklin Roosevelt, whose vision of the New Deal, the Four Freedoms, and an Economic Bill of Rights clearly trumps the former figures in terms of the pursuit of National Greatness – not to mention that FDR's 12-year presidency entailed the making of the Greatest Generation, the most progressive generation in American history.

But far more tragically, the right apparently took hold of Brooks's argument about "It almost doesn't matter what great task government sets for itself..." – and took us right into Iraq.

Now – in response to an essay by Mark Lilla in *The New Republic*, "The Truth About Our Libertarian Age: Why the Dogma of Democracy Doesn't Always Work" (June 17, 2014) – Brooks returns to the question of America's purpose and promise. However, in contrast to his earlier piece, "The Spiritual Recession: Is America Losing Faith in Universal Democracy?" is not exactly a call for action. It is a lament – a lament that Americans "have lost faith in their own gospel." Which was? That the United States has a mission: "When the U.S. was a weak nation, Americans dedicated themselves to proving that democracy could last. When the U.S. became a superpower, Americans felt responsible for creating a global order that would nurture the speed of democracy." But today, he says, "The nation is tired, distrustful, divided and withdrawing. Democratic vistas give way to laissez-faire fatalism: History has no shape. The dream of universal democracy seems naive. National interest matters most."

In conclusion, holding left and right equally responsible for the loss of faith, he observes worryingly that "if America isn't a champion of universal democracy, what is the country for?"

Again, it is easy to take apart Brooks's argument. It not only makes no direct reference to how the Bush administration lied us into a war in Iraq. No less crucially, it also makes no reference to the 40-year-long war from above that the right and conservative rich have pursued against working people – all too often with the deference of Democrats – and how that class war has gutted the middle class; threatened, in places suppressed, the rights of workers, women, and minorities; and restored Gilded Age inequalities of wealth and power. And yet, for all of that, we should not ignore Brooks's question: "What is America for?"

As the state of the nation, not to mention our own distance from political power and influence, attest, we too have failed to answer that question in a compelling way. We have lost touch with the progressive tradition that articulated and sustained the vision of America as a grand experiment in freedom, equality, and democracy. And as a consequence, we have for too long allowed the right to redefine America's purpose and promise in favor of empowering and enriching corporations and the propertied and suppressing or dampening popular democratic hopes, aspirations, and energies.

Indeed, if we truly want to build a populist majority – if we truly want, as FDR put it in 1930, "to make America fairly radical for a generation" – if we truly want to enhance American democratic life and prosperity for all, then we must answer Brooks's question. Recent progressive victories are encouraging, but the majority of Americans are still waiting to hear what we have to say. We need to articulate America's democratic purpose and promise anew and remind ourselves and our fellow citizens what it means to be an American.

9

The Progressive Vision of American Exceptionalism

In the spring of 2014, the Wisconsin Public Radio/National Public Radio show **To the Best of Our Knowledge** *asked several writers if they had a "Dangerous Idea" they would like to talk about (unscripted). Mine was American exceptionalism. But I did not speak on the dangers of the right-wing rendition of it. I spoke on the original idea of American exceptionalism – which is dangerous because it demands progressive action and struggle to realize. The following – published at Moyers and Company on July 1, 2014 – is a slightly edited version of my remarks:*

American exceptionalism sounds like a very conservative idea, right?

But you know what? For more than 200 years, American exceptionalism was a radical idea. It was an idea of liberals and progressives. It was an idea that didn't say "we are superior" – that we have all the answers. No, it was an idea about what America could be, should be and, if we act on it, would be.

Think back to the words of Thomas Paine in *Common Sense* – "We have it in our power to begin the world over again" – and to his call for the creation of an unprecedented democratic republic. Think about the Founders, the writing of the Declaration of Independence, and Thomas Jefferson's words "We hold these Truths to be self-evident, that all Men are created equal, that they are endowed by their Creator with certain unalienable Rights, that among these are Life, Liberty and the Pursuit of Happiness—That to secure these rights, Governments are instituted among Men, deriving their just powers from the Consent of the Governed."

And recall the Framers' Preamble to the US Constitution. We hear about the Constitution's conservatism. And yet those first three words, "We the People" – those are radical words.

Those kinds of words provided American life with democratic imperative. They embedded a democratic impulse in American life.

You know, there's a democratic spirit inside almost all Americans.

The democratic idea of American exceptionalism insisted that We the People can govern – that we don't need kings and aristocrats – that we can govern ourselves. And that we can govern ourselves not only politically, but also that we can govern ourselves economically and culturally.

And then think about the generations of Americans empowered by that argument, that vision, that promise: the freethinkers, the abolitionists, the women's rights advocates, agrarian populists, the labor unionists, the civil rights campaigners.... Those folks believed in American exceptionalism and they used that belief – which they knew they shared with their fellow citizens – to challenge their fellow citizens to make America freer, more equal and more democratic.

That idea of American exceptionalism didn't see American progress as natural or inevitable, but it was compelling. That idea of American exceptionalism empowered generations to make America better – to recognize that we are a grand experiment in democracy, and the only way you can carry out an experiment is to test its limits.

Now, something obviously went wrong. Today, when you hear the argument about American exceptionalism, it's almost always a conservative argument – you know, it's not about life, liberty and the pursuit of happiness, but about life, liberty and the pursuit of property – that is, protect property, limit government. It's not about democracy; it's about individualism, power, and profits.

And yet, even sadder than that — because we've always heard conservatives argue that kind of thing – is that, at best, we are told we have to defend what exists, not advance what exists.

But of course, the saddest thing is that liberals and progressives seem embarrassed by the idea of American exceptionalism, because they, we, have somehow allowed ourselves to believe that an argument for American exceptionalism is an argument for American superiority, an argument that claims "we have all the answers."

We need to remember that American exceptionalism – as radicals and progressives such as Thomas Paine, Walt Whitman, Herman Melville, Eugene Debs, Franklin and Eleanor Roosevelt, and Martin Luther King saw it – is a challenge to enhance freedom, equality, and democracy. Indeed, the danger is that if we forget that dangerous idea, we will cease to be Americans.

So, we progressives should redeem it.

10

The Rich's Class Warfare is Winning – or *What the Fuck Happened?*

Published at The Daily Beast, March 16, 2015

Reading Steve Fraser's *The Age of Acquiescence* brought to mind a note that a young woman student had appended to a final essay exam in one of my classes some twenty-five years ago. After doing a splendid job of answering the question posed, she proceeded to explain that she had decided to drop her major in our academic program Social Change and Development (now titled *Democracy and Justice Studies*). As she saw it, in the light of all she had read in our courses about the "power and hegemony" of the nation's political, economic, and military elites – what radical sociologist C. Wright Mills had dubbed *The Power Elite* – the smartest thing for her to do was to sign up for the Business major. What she had learned, she said, had angered her, but it also had convinced her that there really was very little she and others of her generation could do to make a critical difference. So, "If you can't beat them, you might as well join them."

What my student wrote in her note forced me to think anew about what my professorial colleagues and I were actually doing in our courses – for our declared mission has always been to teach students to not only know about the making of America and the modern world, but also consider how they themselves as citizens might "make history" today. Her words made me ask if we were focusing too much on "structures of power and wealth" and "dominant ideologies" and too little on popular aspirations, ideas, and actions? I did not want us to cultivate fantasies and delusions in our students. But I sure as hell didn't want us to cultivate pessimism and cynicism. As I saw it, we needed to make sure that our majors recognized how generations of Americans had actually succeeded in making American life freer, more equal, and more democratic. Otherwise, they might lack the insights, imagination, and inspiration that enable, encourage, and *empower* democratic initiatives.

After reading *The Age of Acquiescence*, I wondered if I too ought not head over to the Business School. I exaggerate, of course. But I kid you not when I say that by the time you put down Fraser's book you may very well feel not just angry, but also quite depressed. Though I should note that it didn't help that I was reviewing it at the very same time that Wisconsin Governor Scott Walker and his GOP comrades in the state legislature – having already stripped public employees of their collective bargaining rights in 2011 – were now pursuing the further Dixiefication of the Badger State by not only drastically cutting the budget of the University of Wisconsin System, but also hurriedly turning Wisconsin into a "Right-to-Work" state.

An award-winning labor historian for his 1991 biography of union leader Sidney Hillman, *Labor Will Rule*; a co-founder of Scholars, Artists, and Writers for Social Justice (SAWSJ), a late-1990s initiative of progressive intellectuals that sought to place labor's cause back on the public agenda (a campaign I also joined in organizing); and for some years now a leading historian of Wall Street, Fraser has produced a very critical and powerful work on the state of American capitalism and democracy. In fact, if you really want to learn about the making of the inequalities of power and wealth that we suffer, leave Thomas Piketty's *Capital in the Twenty-First Century* on the coffee table and pick up Fraser's new book. But again, don't expect to be inspired.

In *The Age of Acquiescence*, Fraser addresses the question that so many of us on the left have been agonizing over for some time: Why do Americans remain so seemingly passive in the face of forty years of class war from above? A class war from above that has subordinated the public good to private greed, concentrated power and wealth, sent vast numbers of working people into the ranks of the "working poor," and subjected democratic politics to "plutocratic" control. A class war from above that has engendered nothing less than a Second Gilded Age.

How can it be, Fraser asks? Historically, Americans were anything but politically passive. In the first Gilded Age – as Mark Twain titled the late nineteenth century in his first novel – farmers, workers, and even middle-class folk continually rose up, organized, and not only called for an "American standard of living." Striking fear in the hearts and minds of the nation's political and economic elites, they also demanded laws to limit the power of capital and empower democratic government to lay the groundwork for a "Cooperative Commonwealth." How can it be that we do not see such struggles and hear such calls today? "America's history," Fraser observes, "is mysterious in just this way." Or as my own dear book editor once put it – demanding that I agree to try and answer it before he would actually issue me a contract – *What the fuck happened?*

Fraser divides his work into two parts: Part One – "Class Warfare in America: The Long Nineteenth Century" – tells the story of the original Gilded Age. And Part Two – "Desire and Fear in the Second Gilded Age" – tells that of our own.

As Fraser observes in his Introduction, for all of the accumulation of power and wealth that characterizes both ages, the two are fundamentally different. It's not just that "The first Gilded Age, despite its glaring inequities, was accompanied by a gradual rise in the standard of living; the second by its gradual erosion." No, it's much more than that.

As he presents it: Whereas "Profitability during the first... rested first of all on transforming the resources of preindustrial societies into marketable commodities produced by wage laborers... Profitability during the second...relied instead on cannibalizing the industrial edifice erected during the first, and exporting the results of capital liquidation to the four corners of the earth..." And our vaunted "Prosperity, once driven by cost-cutting mechanization and technological breakthroughs, came instead to rest uneasily on oceans of consumer and corporate debt." Moreover, while in the first Gilded Age, "the work ethic constituted the nuclear core of American cultural belief and practice," in the second, we have "an economy kept aloft by finance and mass consumption [based] on an ethos of immediate gratification."

Fraser seeks the answer to America's pressing mystery in those differences: "Can these two diverging political economies – one resting on industry, the other on finance – and these two polarized sensibilities – one fearing God, the other living in an impromptu moment to moment – explain the Great Noise of the first Gilded Age and the Great Silence of the second?"

Delivered with real verve, the first part of *The Age of Acquiescence* reminded me of the best work of Karl Marx. Like Marx in the *Communist Manifesto* and *Capital*, but from an American perspective, Fraser writes majestically if not almost poetically about the making of capitalism. He offers a sweeping narrative of the violent and tragic upheavals that constituted the primitive accumulation of capital, the dramatic and promising technological innovations and transformations of the industrial revolution, and the unprecedented concentrations of power and wealth that resulted. And his chapters on the "Second Civil Wars" of the post-Civil War decades are no less dynamic. Here he reminds us of how the nation's rural and urban laboring classes, both native-born and immigrant, organized as Populists, Labor-unionists, Socialists, and Anarchists (not to mention Progressives), sought to resist, reform, and/or bring an end to the exploitations and oppressions that they suffered and made the ascendant Captains of Industry truly fearful of an impending radical-democratic Apocalypse.

Moreover, along the way Fraser does a nice job of exposing the historical realities that are often obscured in politicians' speeches and pundits' ravings about the making of American greatness. For example, while the celebrated Homestead Act of 1862 may well have afforded Midwestern landholdings to millions of aspiring agrarians, it also ended up underwriting the emergence of railway magnates whose business networks and empires took "good advantage" of those very same yeomen family-farmers when they sought to send their harvests to urban markets. Consider the fact that "As early as 1862, two-thirds of Iowa (or ten million acres) was owned by speculators." And in that same vein, Fraser notes how the abolition of slavery down in Dixie did not bring an end to coercive labor systems. All too soon, Southern planters and their law enforcers took to subjecting vast numbers of poor blacks and whites to sharecropping, debt peonage, and chain gangs.

Fraser's story of "the long nineteenth-century" closes in the early 1930s with the Crash of 1929 and the ensuing Great Depression. However, as he points out, it was not simply the collapse of capitalism that brought the curtain down on the Gilded Age, but all the more the political doing of Democratic President Franklin Roosevelt, his New Dealers, and especially a resurgent labor movement. Together, if not always in tandem, they harnessed the accumulated legacy of generations of struggle to launch the liberal, indeed, social-democratic, labors and campaigns of the 1930s. Unfortunately, however, Fraser does not adequately relate here how the radical-democratic ideas, solidarities, initiatives, and struggles of the New Deal provided the propulsion not only for a democratic economic recovery and a progressive political revolution, but also for the nation's war effort against Fascism, postwar democratic action right through the 1960s, *and* our own sense of the possible, if not imperative, today.

A critical weakness of *The Age of Acquiescence* – which because of all the energy that fuels the first part of the book does not become apparent until the second part – is that it does not give sufficient attention to popular politics and thought. Gilded Age movements emerged and took up the fight and liberal and radical intellectuals wrote books and proposed schemes. But American working people themselves weren't just fighting against the concentration of power and wealth; they were also fighting *for* America.

So, what drove and inspired them to rally, join together, and do battle against corporate exploitation and oppression? From where did the idea of a Cooperative Commonwealth emanate? While Fraser does not completely ignore the legacy and memory of the American Revolution, he does not make enough of how generations of Americans came to not only feel and regularly renew the democratic imperative and impulse that the Revolution gave to American life, but also, believing in America's exceptional promise and possibilities, continually endeavored to make real the vision of the nation projected in Thomas Paine's *Common Sense,* the Declaration, and the Constitution and Bill of Rights, and rearticulated in Lincoln's Gettysburg Address and FDR's Four Freedoms.

As a consequence, while Fraser goes on in the latter half of the work to render a powerful indictment of financial capitalism, the political-economic and cultural order it has created, and what it is doing to us, he ultimately fails to appreciate the persistence of that democratic spirit and what we might make of it.

Fraser does proceed to tell us an awful lot about what is going down. With real panache, he details the weapons, ideas, myths, and fear mongering that the right and rich have wielded against Americans. Perhaps too much so, for at times one gets the feeling that he is merely updating the decidedly elitist mass-culture criticism of the 1950s. Sure, what he says is far more radical and anti-capitalist in content and tone. But he gets awfully close to calling us all "cheerful robots" as the politically frustrated C. Wright Mills ended up doing in 1960 in his otherwise wonderful book *The Sociological Imagination. Yes,* our Captains of Consciousness with their amazing corporate powers of persuasion have used the wonders and delights of consumerism to tantalize, distract, and, quite possibly, pacify us. And yet, as Fraser himself makes clear along the way, politics does matter.

Thus, he also recounts how conservatives did a helluva job in the late 1940s and early 1950s wielding the Cold War and McCarthyism against not just American communists (whose total numbers were always limited), but also, and all the more critically, the entire American left. How, aided by a resurgent right, corporate chiefs in the early 1970s rallied and declared war on working people. And even more sadly, how, over and over again since the 1970s, the so-called Party of the People, the Democratic Party – led by Carter, Clinton, and now Obama – has proffered "Hope and Change" but afforded a politics in office which has left American workers hanging.

Nonetheless. Fraser shortchanges the popular democratic spirit that, however disappointed and subdued it may have become, continues to run through American life and – let's face it – helped to fuel the explosive rise of the Tea Party.

Revealing that he has not yet fully descended into the Inferno and abandoned all hope, Fraser actually opened *The Age of Acquiescence* by referring to the sudden eruption in 2011 of the Occupy Wall Street movement (OWS). And in closing his Introductory remarks he asks if perhaps the Age of Acquiescence is coming to a close: "Is [OWS] a turning point in our country's history? Have we reached the limits of auto-cannibalism? Is capitalism any longer compatible with democracy? Was it ever?" But he makes practically nothing of a potentially more radical, inspiring, and hope-inducing series of events in which American working people actually fought back.

In the winter and spring of 2011 – well before OWS – upwards of 100,000 Wisconsin workers and their families rose up and repeatedly turned out, marched around, and occupied the state capitol building in Madison with grand hopes of blocking Republican Governor Scott Walker from stripping public employees of their hard-won collective bargaining rights. *And do please remember that Wisconsin in 1959 was the first state to enact such rights.*

We were not shopping. We were showing those who had forgotten it, or forsaken it, that *"This is what democracy looks like."* And with good reason we imagined that the President whom we had done so much to elect would "march" with us – for he had promised in 2008 that he would don his walking shoes to do so whenever workers' rights were threatened. But he did not. And not only did Scott Walker and Company win that battle, but now, just this past week, Walker signed the Right-to-Work bill. Surprisingly, labor historian Fraser makes little of the Wisconsin Rising. He simply notes that it was just another example of the right and conservative rich whittling away at workers' rights. We, however, will not forget what democracy looks like.

For all he says of the abiding power of the powerful, Fraser expects and looks forward to a new age of populism... And I do too. But if we are to redeem America's promise and renew the fight for freedom, equality, and democracy, we must appreciate, grasp onto, and make more of our fellow citizens' persistent democratic spirit.

We need to write histories and arguments that enable our fellow citizens to recognize not only how they are being screwed, but also *why being screwed bothers them so and what they might do about it.* In that fashion we will cultivate an historical memory and imagination that re-energizes America's democratic impulse and encourages and empowers popular democratic action. Otherwise, we might as well all head across campus to be schooled by Business.

11

"Life, Liberty, and the Pursuit of Happiness" Demands $15 an Hour

Published at Moyers and Company, April 27, 2015

Knowing that "necessitous men are not free men," President Franklin D. Roosevelt launched a New Deal in 1933 that rallied Americans to not only fight the Great Depression, but also to combat poverty, reduce inequality, and enhance American democratic life.

Together, President and People subjected the banks and national commerce to government supervision, provided jobs for the jobless, and refurbished the nation's infrastructure and environment.

Moreover, right from the start, FDR and his New Dealers in the Cabinet and Congress set out to establish a minimum wage and empower workers to organize unions.

When the majority of Americans called for further action, FDR and his allies launched a Second New Deal in 1935 that increased corporate regulation and taxes, expanded public works and employment, created a social security system, and bolstered workers' capacities to secure industrial democracy in their workplaces. All of which enabled Americans to not only confront the Depression, but also go on to win the Second World War and turn the United States into the strongest and most prosperous nation in history.

How many times must we say it? We need to do what FDR and our parents and grandparents did. We need to launch a new New Deal. We need to regulate and tax capital, refurbish the national infrastructure and environment, and empower workers to cultivate economic democracy and reduce inequality. But to do all of that we need to expand our already-resurgent progressive populist movement in favor of a new politics in 2016.

For starters, we need to press President Obama and Congress to raise the minimum wage to $15 an hour. At the least we must push the President and aspiring Democratic candidates to "take a note" from FDR and set a progressive-populist political agenda for the upcoming campaigns.

Declaring that "economic laws are not made by nature [but] by human beings," Roosevelt told his fellow citizens in the presidential campaign of 1932 that it was time for a new "economic declaration of rights" to renew the nation's democratic promise of "life, liberty, and the pursuit of happiness" – the promise proclaimed by the Founders in the Declaration of Independence of 1776.

As FDR put it: "Every man has a right to life; and this means he also has a right to make a comfortable living... Our government...owes to everyone an avenue to possess himself of a portion of [America's] plenty sufficient for his needs through his work." And with good reason, Americans would elect him to the presidency four times.

Defeating Republican incumbent Herbert Hoover, Roosevelt and his New Dealers quickly secured from Congress an extraordinary series of relief, recovery, and reconstruction initiatives. They made many a terrible and tragic mistake, but they continually empowered working people. The National Industrial Recovery Act of 1933 (NIRA) set up Labor and Consumer Advisory Boards, licensed workers to organize unions, and established the first national minimum wage. But as Roosevelt saw it, a minimum wage was not enough. He looked forward to setting a "living wage." In fact, on signing the Act he said: "no business which depends for its existence on paying less than living wages has any right to continue in this country." And he meant it – which was one of the reasons corporate bosses hated him.

Indeed, Roosevelt – who said he welcomed the hatred of the 1 percent (the "economic royalists") – believed in workers' rights to organize and he knew that economic recovery and growth depended on raising workers' purchasing power.

When big business resisted workers' organizing efforts, FDR showed his support for the cause of labor. In 1934 he came to Green Bay, Wisconsin – just 60 miles north of the town of Kohler, where workers had gone out on strike against the Kohler Corporation – and there he spoke of how generations of working people had had to fight for their rights and were continuing to do so. And in 1935 he put his words into action and signed into law the National Labor Relations Act (NLRA – *aka* the "Wagner Act" for its great author Senator Robert Wagner) – which placed the federal government solidly behind the struggle for union representation and collective bargaining. The battles for industrial democracy continued. But workers were now backed in their efforts by the federal government.

Speaking at the dedication of a war memorial in St. Louis in 1936, FDR not only put into words the purpose of the New Deal and the struggles underway. He also redefined American patriotism for a generation: "A true patriotism urges us to build an even more substantial America where the good things of life may be shared by more of us, where the social injustices will not be encouraged to flourish."

Even when conservative Republicans and reactionary Southern Democrats had enough combined seats in Congress to block or water down progressive legislative initiatives, FDR and his congressional allies fought to enact laws that would raise workers' wages and guarantee their rights. And in 1938, despite corporate and conservative opposition, they secured passage of the Fair Labor Standards Act (FLSA), which abolished child labor and established both a minimum wage and overtime pay for at least one in four American workers.

Even then, however, President Roosevelt did not stop. He regularly called for expanding Social Security and for enacting programs to assure housing and healthcare coverage to all Americans. Most dramatically, in January 1941 – less than a year before their entry into World War II – he articulated Americans' finest aspirations in a vision, or promise, of four fundamental freedoms: "Freedom of speech and expression, Freedom of worship, Freedom from want, Freedom from fear." And when Americans' "rendezvous with destiny" came, FDR – for all his terrible faults and failings on race – made sure to work with labor to advance both the war effort and workers' rights and needs.

Though both the AFL and the CIO had issued "no strike pledges" in the wake of Pearl Harbor, he knew he too had to act to tame capital and sustain industrial peace. Scrapping prewar arrangements, he set up the National War Labor Board (NWLB) in January 1942 and accorded equal representation at all levels of its operations to both business and labor. Assigned responsibility for settling war-industry disputes and setting war-industry wages, the NWLB announced not only the "Little Steel Formula," which granted labor a 15 percent cost-of-living increase to cover the rate of inflation since January 1941 and effectively set a pattern for all industries, but also a "Maintenance of Membership" policy whereby unions that honored the "no strike pledge" would automatically enroll new workers as members for the duration of their existing contracts, unless those workers themselves opted out in their first two weeks on the job. Propelled by the Maintenance of Membership rules in the war industries and organizing campaigns elsewhere, unions would expand their ranks during the war from 10 million to 15 million – with women's memberships increasing from 800,000 to 3 million.

Notably, while corporate profits would increase during

the war, class inequalities would actually decrease due to the administration's taxation and wage-and-price-control policies as well as to the concerted efforts of the expanding labor and consumer movements. While the top fifth of family incomes would grow by 20 percent, those below them grew even faster, the bottom two-fifths by more than 60 percent. As labor historian Nelson Lichtenstein has noted: "Working people ate better and worried less... infant mortality declined by more than one-third...[and] life expectancy surged ahead by three years for whites and by five for African Americans."

Even as America was fighting Fascism and Imperialism in the name of the Four Freedoms, corporate capitalists and conservatives resisted FDR's pro-labor initiatives – compelling workers to stage many a walk-out in protest at management practices. But Roosevelt continued to project the promise of the Four Freedoms. And in January 1944 – when surveys revealed that Americans wanted to pursue a host of grand social- and industrial-democratic initiatives at war's end – the President went before Congress and called for enactment of an "economic bill of rights" that would assure all Americans "an American standard of living higher than ever before known."

Recalling the arguments he made in 1932, Roosevelt said: "This Republic had its beginning, and grew to its present strength, under the protection of certain inalienable political rights... They were our rights to life and liberty. As our Nation has grown in size and stature, however – as our industrial economy expanded – these political rights proved inadequate to assure us equality in the pursuit of happiness." But he continued: "We have come to a clear realization of the fact that true individual freedom cannot exist without economic security and independence. 'Necessitous men are not free men.'"

Evoking Jefferson, the Founders, and Lincoln, he contended that, "In our day these economic truths have become accepted as self-evident," and, "We have accepted, so to speak, a second Bill of Rights under which a new basis of security and prosperity can be established for all regardless of station, race, or creed." This Second Bill of Rights included:

The right to a useful and remunerative job in the industries or shops or farms or mines of the Nation;

The right to earn enough to provide adequate food and clothing and recreation;

The right of every farmer to raise and sell his products at a return which will give him and his family a decent living;

The right of every businessman, large and small, to trade in an atmosphere of freedom from unfair competition and domination by monopolies at home or abroad;

The right of every family to a decent home;

The right to adequate medical care and the opportunity to achieve and enjoy good health;

The right to adequate protection from the economic fears of old age, sickness, accident, and unemployment;

The right to a good education.

In sum, he stated: "All of these rights spell security. And after this war is won we must be prepared to move forward, in the implementation of these rights, to new goals of human happiness and well-being."

However, as much as Americans wanted it, the Second Bill of Rights was not enacted. But FDR did secure – with the support, ironically enough, of the ever-conservative American Legion – a decidedly social-democratic GI Bill to enable millions of veterans to rebuild themselves and America.

The legacy of the FDR years lived on... A generation – the Greatest Generation – did not give up what it had accomplished. They fully embraced Social Security and in the course of the immediate postwar years, and then the Great Society campaigns of the 1960s, they expanded it both to cover those previously excluded and to include healthcare for the elderly and poor (Medicare and Medicaid). And even though Republicans and Southern Democrats severely hamstrung labor's capacity to organize by passing the 1947 Taft-Hartley Act (which allowed states to enact right to work laws), unions continued to expand and in the 1960s and early 1970s public employee unionism dramatically took off.

Taxes were high. Wages grew. The economy boomed. Civic action and high voter turnout were the norm. Public investments and progressive public policies made for a better America. And both inequality and poverty decreased.

Let's not get nostalgic... After forty years of class war from above, Reaganomics, and Austerity, we have much to do to renew the Fight for the Four Freedoms.

Recalling FDR, let's remind our fellow citizens that "economic laws are not made by nature [but] by human beings" – that "no business which depends for its existence on paying less than living wages has any right to continue in this country" – and that "A true patriotism urges us to build an even more substantial America where the good things of life may be shared by more of us, where the social injustices will not be encouraged to flourish."

And then let's start making history by winning the fight for $15.

12

Social Democracy Is 100-Percent American

Published at Moyers and Company, July 3, 2015

Appearing late last week on MSNBC's *Morning Joe*, Senator Claire McCaskill of Missouri insisted that Democratic presidential candidate Senator Bernie Sanders of Vermont "is too liberal to gather enough votes in this country to become president." Indeed, responding to the fact that candidate Sanders is not only drawing big, enthusiastic crowds to campaign events in Iowa and New Hampshire, but also pulling within 10 points of frontrunner and party favorite Hillary Clinton in certain state polls, McCaskill said: "It's not unusual for someone who has an extreme message to have a following."

Extreme? McCaskill's remarks indicate that we may be in more trouble than we thought. For some time we have feared that Republican politicians were losing their minds. Now it seems we must worry, as well, that Democratic politicians are losing their memories.

Clearly, McCaskill's attack – which, to me, smacked of red baiting – was intended as a dismissal of Bernie Sanders's candidacy based on the fact that Sanders, who has repeatedly won elections in Vermont as an independent and then caucused with the Senate Democrats, is a self-described "democratic socialist" or "social democrat." And of course, we all know that social democracy is not just unpopular in the United States, it is *un-American*.

Well, think again. Social democracy is 100-percent American. We may be latecomers to recognizing a universal right to health care (indeed, we are not quite there yet). But we were first in creating a universal right to public education, in endowing ourselves with ownership of national parks, and, for that matter, in conferring voting rights on males without property and abolishing religious tests for holding national office.

But there's even more to the story. It was the American Revolution's patriot and pamphleteer, Thomas Paine — a hero today to folks left and right, including tea partiers — who launched the social-democratic tradition in the 1790s. In his pamphlets, *Rights of Man* and *Agrarian Justice*, Paine outlined plans for combating poverty that would become what we today call Social Security.

As Paine put it in the latter work, since God has provided the earth and the land upon it as a collective endowment for humanity, those who have come to possess the land as private property owe the *dispossessed* an annual rent for it. Specifically, Paine delineated a limited redistribution of income by way of a tax on landed wealth and property. The funds collected were to provide both grants for young people to get started in life and pensions for the elderly.

Think again. The social-democratic tradition was nurtured by Americans both immigrant and native-born: By the so-called "sewer socialist" German Americans who helped to build the Midwest and, inspired by the likes of Eugene Debs and Victor Berger, radically improved urban life by winning battles for municipal ownership of public utilities. By the Jewish and Italian workers who toiled and suffered in the sweatshops of New York and Chicago but then, led by David Dubinsky and Sidney Hillman, created great labor unions such as the International Ladies Garment Workers Union and the Amalgamated Clothing Workers of America. By the farmers and laborers who rallied to the grand encampments on the prairies organized by populists and socialists across the southwest to hear how, working together in alliances, they could break the grip of Wall Street and create a Cooperative Commonwealth. *And* by African-Americans who came north in the Great Migration to build new lives for themselves and, led by figures such as the socialist, labor leader and civil rights activist A. Philip Randolph, energized the civil rights movement in the 1930s.

And yes, think again. Think about the greatest president of the 20th century, Franklin Roosevelt, whose grand, social-democratic New Deal initiatives – from the CCC, WPA and Rural Electrification Administration, to Social Security and the National Labor Relations Act — not only rescued the nation from the Great Depression, but also reduced inequality and poverty and helped ready the United States to win the Second World War and become the strongest and most prosperous nation on earth.

Moreover, those we celebrate as the Greatest Generation, the men and women who confronted the Great Depression and went on to defeat fascism, fought for the decidedly social-democratic Four Freedoms – freedom of speech and religion, freedom from want and fear – and the chance of realizing them at war's end.

Polls conducted in 1943 showed that 94 percent of Americans endorsed old-age pensions; 84 percent, job insurance; 83 percent, universal national health insurance; and 79 percent, aid for students — leading FDR in his 1944 State of the Union message to propose a Second Bill of Rights that would guarantee those very things to all Americans. All of which would be blocked by a conservative coalition of pro-corporate Republicans and white supremacist southern Democrats. And yet, with the aid of the otherwise conservative American Legion, FDR did secure one of the greatest social-democratic programs in American history: the GI Bill that enabled 12,000,000 returning veterans to progressively transform themselves and the nation for the better.

Nor did that generation of veterans give up their social-democratic aspirations. On reaching middle age in the 1960s, they enacted civil rights, voting rights, Medicare and Medicaid; established protections for the environment, workers and consumers; *and* dramatically expanded educational opportunities, especially in public higher education.

We ourselves honor America's social-democratic history with two great monuments on the National Mall – not just the FDR Memorial, but also the Martin Luther King Jr. Memorial. Yes, King was a democratic socialist. Drawing on the New Deal experience, embracing the American tradition of Christian socialism and peaceful activism, and believing, like so many of his generation, that Americans could harness the powers of democratic government to enhance freedom and equality, he campaigned for both racial justice and the rights of working people and the poor.

Senator McCaskill's attack on Senator Sanders appears to have been launched on behalf of the Clinton campaign. Its rationale rests on the belief that, in the light of the past 40 years of conservative ascendancy and liberal retreat, her words were simple common sense: *Aren't we, as the talking heads tell us, a center-right nation?*

Well, no, we are emphatically not. And it is regrettable that by swallowing this myth, the present leadership of the Democratic Party, embodied in the Democratic National Committee, has, in election after election, shrunk from some of the party's best traditions in order to keep up in the race for campaign cash, even to the extent of marginalizing and openly scorning what is described as its "left wing."

Indeed, when America's purpose and promise have been in jeopardy we acted radically, progressively, and, yes, as social democrats. Hillary Clinton herself seemed to recognize the power of that history and its legacy by launching her new presidential campaign at New York City's Four Freedoms Park on Roosevelt Island. Though she never did actually pronounce the words of FDR's Four Freedoms, her speech revealed some awareness of a reviving — dare we say it? — social-democratic spirit. Whether simply tactical or genuine on her part is an important question that remains to be answered.

Bernie Sanders may never appear at Four Freedoms Park. But he often sounds like FDR, not simply because you can practically hear him saying of the one percent what FDR did – "I welcome their hatred" – but all the more because of what he wants to do: tax the rich, create a single-payer national health care system, make public higher education free to all qualified students, create jobs by refurbishing the nation's public infrastructure, and address the environment and climate change.

But even more critically, like FDR, he doesn't say he wants to fight for us. He seeks to encourage the fight in us: "It is up to us to launch the most heroic of all struggles: a political revolution." If that is "extreme," then Democrats like McCaskill are not just forgetting their history. They are trying to suppress it.

That Sanders, given his background, is garnering huge crowds who shout his name with an enthusiasm reminiscent of the heyday of the People's Party in the 1890s, radiates a special glow. Americans may once again be remembering who they are and what they need to do to recapture a government now in thrall to the Money Power. And that ain't extreme. It's fundamentally American.

13

This Generation, Too, Has a Rendezvous with Destiny: A Progressive Commencement Speech

I delivered the following speech as the Winter Commencement Address at the University of Wisconsin-Green Bay on December 19, 2015. And in February 2016 it was published in **Vital Speeches of the Day.**

Commencement speakers usually call on graduates to embrace the future. But I'm going to call on you to do something else: I am going to urge you to embrace the past.

I want you to remember who you are.

I want you to remember who *we* are.

We are Americans... And I – hopefully, *we* – want you to appreciate what that demands of you in the face of the daunting crises that confront us. Bluntly stated: It is time for you to make history as our greatest generations have made history.

Echoing what President Franklin Roosevelt told my parents' generation in 1936: *I firmly believe that this Generation – your Generation – has a Rendezvous with Destiny.*

True: We do not suffer a Great Depression... True: We do not confront foreign enemies as powerful as Nazi Germany and Imperial Japan... And yet: We do face crises no less challenging.

Think about it. For the past forty years we have subordinated the public good to corporate priorities and private greed. And we have seen our industries decline, our infrastructures decay and collapse, and our environment go haywire.

For the past forty years we have subjected ourselves to ever widening inequalities and ever intensifying insecurities. And we have watched the middle class erode, politics and public life decay, and democracy surrender to plutocracy.

For the past forty years we have denied our own democratic impulses and yearnings. And we have witnessed direct, devastating, and too often deadly assaults on the rights of workers, women, and people of color.

But perhaps worst of all, we seem to have forgotten who we are... And it has made us fearful – as if we were deer caught in headlights – the headlights of history.

Well, enough of that!

It is time that we started remembering. But we need to do more than remember... We also need to act. We need to act both courageously and determinedly.

It is time for you and your generation to transform this nation as generations of Americans did in the 1770s – the 1860s – and the 1930s and 1940s – not to mention the 1960s.

What did those generations do?

They rejected fear and gave real historical meaning – *indeed, historic and transcendent meaning* – to our finest ideals and aspirations:

To Thomas Paine's argument in his revolutionary pamphlet *Common Sense*, that "we have it in our power to begin the world over again";

To Thomas Jefferson's phrases in the Declaration of Independence, that "all men are created equal... endowed by their creator with certain unalienable rights... among these are life, liberty and the pursuit of happiness";

To the Founders' words in the Preamble to the Constitution: "We the people of the United States, in order to form a more perfect union...";

To Abraham Lincoln's lines at Gettysburg in 1863 proclaiming "a new birth of freedom" and insisting upon a "government of the people, by the people, for the people";

To Franklin Roosevelt's call in 1941 to create a nation and a world marked by four fundamental freedoms: "Freedom of speech and expression, Freedom of worship, Freedom from want, Freedom from fear";

And to Martin Luther King Jr.'s pronouncement on the steps of the Lincoln Memorial in 1963: "I have a dream...";

Yes, they were terribly flawed generations.

Nonetheless, for all of their faults and failings, for all of the tragedy and irony that marked their lives, and for all of the exploitation and oppression that they left in place, each of those generations – in all of their marvelous diversity – found it in themselves to rise up, to deal head on with the daunting challenges they faced, and to make America both stronger and richer than ever before.

But that's just the half of it.

The most amazing thing about those generations; the thing that made each of them great; the thing that made America truly exceptional; the thing which we sadly have forgotten – *or,* have been made to forget – is that they actually succeeded in doing all of that *NOT* by giving up or suspending their finest ideals and aspirations, but by harnessing the powers of democratic government and making America freer, more equal, and more democratic than ever before.

In the 1770s, Americans – both native-born and immigrant – not only fought a war for independence. They also rejected kings and aristocrats and created an historically unprecedented democratic republic.

In the 1860s, farmers, workers, and the slaves themselves not only defeated the traitorous Southern Confederacy and sustained the Union. They also redeemed the Declaration's promise by bringing an end to black bondage.

In the 1930s – in the shadows of the Great Depression, the worst economic and social catastrophe in U.S. history – working men and women mobilized. They mobilized not only to reform government, provide relief, pursue economic recovery, transform the American landscape, and rebuild the nation's public infrastructure. But also to fight.

They mobilized in labor unions, housewives' campaigns, and civil rights organizations – to fight for their rights as American citizens against the economic royalists, reactionary politicians, and white supremacists who sought to deny them their rights.

And in the 1940s, they not only went "All Out!" to beat Fascism by turning the country into the Arsenal of Democracy, by creating a military force of 16,000,000 men and women, and by shipping overseas to fight for the Four Freedoms. They also continued to fight for those Four Freedoms at home in the United States.

Moreover, they would not only go on to sustain a Cold War against the Soviet Union, make the United States the most powerful and prosperous nation in human history, and create the American middle class; but also – when challenged by their own children to live up to the promise for which they had fought – set themselves to trying to do so.

In the course of the 1960s: They enacted the Civil Rights and Voting Rights acts. They reformed the nation's immigration laws to once again make America an "asylum for mankind." They expanded Social Security to include Medicare for the elderly and Medicaid for the poor. They empowered public employees to organize and bargain collectively. They passed laws that made the environment, the marketplace, and the workplace *safer* for all of us. *And* they vastly expanded educational and cultural opportunities for all Americans – which included creating this University, the University of Wisconsin-Green Bay, fifty years ago.

Take a moment: Consider how we have tragically failed to sustain their hard-fought-for legacy of prosperity and political, social, and industrial democracy…

Surely, whether you are a liberal or a conservative, you can see that the time has come – the time has come to act as the greatest Americans of the past have acted in the face of mortal crises.

It is time to get up, harness the powers of government, and dramatically – *indeed, radically* – enhance American democratic life.

As our greatest democratic poet Walt Whitman put it: "There must be continual additions to our great experiment of how much liberty society will bear."

Or as the Progressive journalist Henry Demarest Lloyd wrote in 1900: "The price of liberty is something more than eternal vigilance. There must also be eternal advance. We can save the rights we have inherited from our fathers only by winning new ones to bequeath our children."

I will repeat that: *The price of liberty is something more than eternal vigilance. There must also be eternal advance. We can save the rights we have inherited from our fathers only by winning new ones to bequeath our children.*

So, not just for your sake, but for the sake of all of us, I urge you to embrace the past – the past that you may not readily recall, but which I know you carry in your deepest memory and imagination.

EMBRACE AMERICA'S PAST.
REMEMBER WHO YOU ARE.
MAKE AMERICA FREER, MORE EQUAL, AND MORE DEMOCRATIC.

14

Time for Radical Action, Not National Therapy

Published at Moyers and Company on May 3, 2016

Now that Donald Trump has all but officially won the GOP presidential nomination, *New York Times* columnist David Brooks asks in his April 29, 2016 piece, "What are we supposed to do?"

Brooks isn't asking Republican leaders that question. "They seem blithely unaware that this is a Joe McCarthy moment," he writes. "Those who walked with Trump will be tainted forever after for the degradation of standards and the general election slaughter." Rather, Brooks is asking what all of us who are appalled by Trump's rhetoric and behavior are supposed to do about the developments that empowered his candidacy. Trump may very well destroy the Republican Party. But his ascendance, Brooks warns, is a symptom of a far more critical and pressing problem.

With the nation's deepening class divide in mind, Brooks points to "how much pain there is in this country," and describes a sense of personal and national decline and "rampant social isolation" induced in the hearts and minds of too many Americans. Observing that all of this has driven many of them to the populist campaigns of Trump and Bernie Sanders, Brooks argues that we are confronting nothing less than a national crisis of "social trust"; indeed, what author and editor R.R. Reno calls a "crisis of solidarity" that demands our urgent individual and collective action.

Although Brooks ends up proffering all the wrong answers, we should not fail to recognize the significance of what he has to say, for his lamentations and calls for action signal more than he realizes or surely intends us to hear. While his words do not speak directly to the renewal of Americans' democratic energies, the anxieties he expresses should help us see that Americans are not simply pained by the class divide, but also determined to do something about it. Time for us to act.

Brooks fails to acknowledge what or who has actually led us into a Second Gilded Age, placing the American dream out of reach for vast numbers of Americans, and fostering that crisis of solidarity. He makes absolutely no mention of the *class war from above* that has marked American life for the past 40 years – a class war that has placed private greed and profits before the public good and general welfare. Not only has it made the rich exceedingly richer and working people poorer, it also has raised up an oligarchy to keep our democracy in check; laid siege to the hard-won rights of workers, women and African Americans; and devastated the communities, organizations and solidarities they built to make their lives more secure.

Ignoring or avoiding all of that, Brooks fails to appreciate what it may take to redeem the nation and liberate ourselves from the fear, pain and isolation that so many of us endure. As Brooks presents it, the historic task of overcoming the class divide and transcending the crisis of solidarity is to be undertaken not in the classic American fashion of citizens joining together and struggling to enhance freedom, equality, and democracy from the bottom up, but by professional and bourgeois elites working to rebuild social trust and solidarity. He does not call for – or even consider – the possibility of popular radical-democratic action against those who insist to their own benefit that we have reached the end of history. No, he proposes a grand program of national social therapy.

Brooks calls on professional and bourgeois folks, the people with whom he confesses he spends so much of his time, to willfully step out of their comfortable surroundings and get to know those who are in pain. Doing so, he says, will enable them to better understand their fellow citizens, develop compassion for them and cultivate a new, more-inclusive story of America. Bizarrely, he suggests that we might well replace the old, no-longer compelling American story in which "the lone individual…rises from the bottom through pluck and work" with one in which "those who suffer from addiction, broken homes, trauma, prison and loss… triumph over the isolation, social instability and dislocation so common today."

Finally, citing such "national projects" as the WPA and NASA, and even hinting at a national service program, Brooks, showing some independence from the contemporary politics of conservatism, calls for launching both private and public initiatives that could serve to bind people together. And apparently eager to set a good example for his class comrades, Brooks actually promises that instead of dwelling in his column on the lives of bourgeois folk he will now "go out into the pain," and report back.

Brooks tells us we are in crisis, that the nation's deepening social divide has undone the solidarities of the past. Notably, he remains silent both as to how this happened and how those solidarities first developed. Though he cites the 1930s WPA as a program possibly worth emulating, he fails to mention how Americans fought the Great Depression by electing the progressive Democrat Franklin Roosevelt to the presidency and how that president led the fight for recovery, reconstruction, and reform both by launching public works projects to engage their labors in improving the nation and by empowering them to organize unions and collectively confront their bosses.

Brooks also fails to recount how in the course of those industrial struggles millions of Americans learned firsthand about solidarity and trust and not only succeeded in enhancing American democracy and securing better lives for themselves and their families, but also prepared us to beat our fascist enemies in World War II.

One cannot help but imagine that Brooks sees what we see – that growing numbers of Americans are rejecting the appeals of political establishments both right and left – and that seeing it gives him reason to be concerned, if not fearful and pained. Some Americans are angry. Some are hopeful. And yet, for all of their evident and at times antagonistic and vicious differences, the angry and the hopeful do seem to share a determination to confront the treachery of the nation's political and economic elites and bring to an end the class war from above that has denied them their nation's historic promise.

We can do so by articulating the democratic imperative and impulses Americans are beginning to feel once again, and by helping us better remember who we are and what we are capable of doing in the light of the solidarities and achievements of the past. The task for America's intellectuals ought not to be, as Brooks sees it, to work at bridging the class divide, but rather to work at ending it.

15

Keeping the True Faith: Rediscovering America on the National Mall

Posted at OurFuture.org and People's Action, June 10, 2016

Newt Gingrich – the leader of the 1994 "Gingrich Revolution" that gave Republicans control of both houses of Congress for the first time in 40 years, former Speaker of the House, occasional Republican presidential candidate, *and, quite possibly,* Donald Trump's running mate – has just issued a third edition, a 10th Anniversary edition you might say, of his 2006 best-seller, *Rediscovering God in America: Reflections on the Role of Faith in Our Nation's History and Future.* Understandably, progressives have generally ignored the work. But I have followed it from the very beginning, both for personal reasons and, even more critically, because I think we have things to learn from Gingrich's work, though not necessarily the things he intended.

A dozen summers ago my younger daughter had the good fortune of serving as a college intern in the Washington office of U.S. Senator Russell Feingold of Wisconsin. I distinctly recall her telephone call asking me if I thought she should attend a lecture for the congressional interns that evening by Newt Gingrich. She was of a mixed mind about going. But I told her she definitely ought to, not just because he was smart (a Ph.D. in History) and an entertaining speaker (though not of the House!), but also because she really ought to find out what our political antagonists had to say to young people in that presidential election year.

I also clearly recall that she rang again later that night to report that, while she obviously didn't agree with him, it was worth going for Gingrich had given a most curious speech. Specifically, he had spoken of having "discovered God on the National Mall" – by which he did not mean he had been "born (once) again" or that God herself had spoken to him, but, rather, that he had come to see all the more clearly by way of the words and texts inscribed on the walls of the Mall's buildings and monuments both how important God had been in American history and how Americans' belief in and embrace of God and his gifts had helped to make America exceptional.

My daughter's report stuck with me, not just because it was sweet of her to ask my advice, and because I have loved the National Mall ever since my very first visit to the nation's capital as a boy in 1959, but also because, based on what she said, I was terribly impressed by Gingrich's latest project (which actually led me to consider what I would say to young people about the National Mall and its monuments).

I figured that Gingrich more than anyone knew what it took to transform American public discourse. He had proved that in 1994 with his reactionary manifesto, *Contract On America* – oops, I mean *Contract With America*. And he apparently had learned from the right's own idol Ronald Reagan how important it was to engage and reshape American historical memory and imagination in favor of propagating a sense of past, present, and future that would encourage political action – which was exactly what Gingrich was trying to do with his walking tour talk of the National Mall. Ignoring, appropriating, and/or suppressing the revolutionary, radical, and progressive agencies, aspirations, and experiences expressed and memorialized there, he had laid hold of America's foremost "sacred space" and "official public memory" and rendered a decidedly conservative narrative of American history.

My fascination for Gingrich's 2004 talk intensified when, two years later, it appeared in print as *Rediscovering God in America,* a little volume of 160 pages of text and black-and-white photos. I immediately bought a copy. And I wasn't the only one who did. The first two editions sold 100,000 copies. Plus, a handsomely produced film version of the walking tour was to sell 300,000 copies. But I didn't just read the book. Along with Thomas Paine's *Common Sense* (1776), Max Lerner's "It Is Later Than You Think: The Need for a Militant Democracy" (1939), and a collection of Bill Moyers' speeches, I placed it bedside to serve, not as a source of religious inspiration or historiographical insights, but as a constant reminder of what we progressives need to do to – in a decidedly more critical and honest fashion – more effectively engage our fellow citizens in a politics of building a more democratic America.

The latest edition of *Rediscovering God in America* is aesthetically far more impressive than the earlier ones. The book is now not only larger in scale but also replete with color photographs and pictures, as well as a new Foreword and a chapter on the Martin Luther King, Jr. Memorial.

And yet, nothing really has changed. The text affords the same basic walking tour, the same lecture/sermon on God and Faith in American history, and the same assault on liberals and progressives who rightly believe that the words of the First Amendment – "Congress shall make no law respecting an establishment of religion, or prohibiting the free exercise thereof" – demands vigilance and firm adherence to "the separation of church and state."

The opening words of Gingrich's introduction, and the right-wing polemic that runs throughout, remain: "There is no attack on American culture more destructive and more historically dishonest than the secular left's relentless effort to drive God out of the public square."

It is easy to scoff at and debunk the "history" Gingrich offers on his walking tour. For a start, he makes no mention of Thomas Paine's *Common Sense* and how it turned Americans' colonial rebellion into "the Revolution" in no small part by offering a vision of a free America liberated from state churches – a vision that mobilized Presbyterians, Methodists, and Baptists, not to mention many a Catholic and Jew, to enlist in the struggle in hopes of overcoming Anglican authority in the South and Congregational domination in New England.

Outlining a constitution for the nation-to-be, Paine not only wrote that it should include something of a Bill of Rights to guarantee "above all things, the free exercise of religion, according to the dictates of conscience." He also insisted that "As to religion, I hold it to be the indispensable duty of government to protect all conscientious professors thereof, and I know of no other business which government has to do therewith." In short, six months before independence was declared, and thirteen years before the Constitution was agreed upon, strict separation of church and state was fundamental to the cause.

Furthermore, while Gingrich stresses the religiosity of the "Founding Fathers," he refuses to acknowledge just how many of them had turned from Christianity to Deism – not only Thomas Paine, whom he utterly ignores, and not just Thomas Jefferson, whom he begrudgingly recognizes as one, but also Benjamin Franklin, George Washington and a host of others. The foremost proof is in the very document, the Declaration of Independence, which Gingrich himself posits as the fountainhead of American liberty. He repeatedly cites Jefferson's words: "We hold these truths to be self-evident, that all men are created equal, that they are endowed by their Creator with certain unalienable Rights, that among these are Life, Liberty and the pursuit of Happiness." But he spends no time considering the words in the very first sentence of the Declaration: "When in the Course of human events it becomes necessary for one people to dissolve the political bands which have connected them with another and to assume among the powers of the earth, the separate and equal station to which the *Laws of Nature and Nature's God* entitle them, a decent respect to the opinions of mankind requires that they

should declare the causes which impel them to the separation."
(My italics.)

And Gingrich pays almost no attention to the Constitution itself – which is only right, I suppose, for the Founders, however conservative many of them were becoming, smartly saw fit to draft, and advance to the states for their approval, a most radical "Godless Constitution."

Lastly (for I could go on and on in that fashion), Gingrich confuses faith and God. Undeniably, Americans have been a religious people of diverse faiths – and we should never fail to remember that and, yes, teach it as part our history. But to say that most Americans have been believers is one thing. To assert, as Gingrich often seems to do, that God Himself has made American history is another thing. He and everyone else are fully entitled to believe that…and to say it in the public square. But they are not entitled to make that belief a doctrine of the federal or state governments or to make of it an idea to be taught in our public schools, for to do so is to deny the First Amendment. And having said that, we should not fail to teach our children that securing the true meaning of religious liberty has taken generations of struggle by Americans both of diverse faiths and of no faith whatsoever.

Suffice it to say that for all of the evidence that Gingrich cites that the Founders and later figures who are memorialized on the Mall may well have been serious believers – and as much as so many Americans have been God-fearing people – Washington and his comrades created a secular government and then appended a First Amendment to the new Constitution that has saved us at many a crucial moment from suffering the likes of Gingrich and his ilk from turning us into an officially "Christian nation."

Well, then, you might well ask: Why do I think we have things to learn from Gingrich and his *Rediscovering God in America*?

Because the struggle continues. As a recent report by People for the American Way registers, the Religious Right is not simply turning "religious liberty" upside down, but also into a "weapon" to be wielded against freedom and equality. And around the country social conservatives are doing their damnedest to blow new holes in the wall separating church and state. In Iowa, they actually succeeded in having the Republican governor endorse a Christian Bible-reading marathon with an official proclamation calling upon citizens of the state to "read the Bible on a daily basis…until the Lord comes."

But we need to attend to Gingrich's work not simply because it offers a rendition of history that bolsters such reactionary campaigns, but also because it reminds us of the imperative of speaking to American historical memory and imagination. We have mastered the art of debunking. We now need to make good use of all the good critical historical studies that left academics have produced on popular struggles for freedom, equality, and democracy. We need to articulate a narrative that reminds Americans who they are and what that demands. Without forgetting the exploitation and oppression that has marked American life, we might also want to take a walk on the Mall to remind ourselves of our revolutionary, radical and progressive past.

16

Let Them Call Us Rebels – We Are All the Heirs of Thomas Paine

Published at Moyers and Company on January 12, 2017

In December 1776, during the darkest days of the Revolution, Thomas Paine wrote the first of his *American Crisis* papers. Following devastating defeats by British forces in Brooklyn and Manhattan, George Washington and the Continental Army were retreating across New Jersey to the Delaware River and Pennsylvania. Paine rode with them, determined to continue the fight and defiantly reaffirming his disgust for Great Britain's King George III.

"Let them call me rebel and welcome," Paine wrote, "I feel no concern from it; but I should suffer the misery of devils, were I to make a whore of my soul by swearing allegiance to one whose character is that of a sottish, stupid, stubborn, worthless, brutish man." The greatest journalist of the Revolution knew how to call out the enemy.

Only 11 months earlier, Paine had published *Common Sense*, a pamphlet of just 50 pages that would turn the world upside down. Calling on Americans to recognize that they were *Americans* not Britons, and that they were fighting not for British rights but for universal human rights, Paine — through words such as "The sun never shined on a cause of greater worth" and "The cause of America is in a great measure the cause of all mankind" — emboldened his fellow citizens-to-be to turn their colonial rebellion into a revolutionary war for independence and to make for themselves and their children a historically unprecedented democratic republic.

Now, however, it seemed America's cause was to collapse on

the frozen fields of Tory-dominated New Jersey. Encouraged by Gen. Washington himself, Paine began to write again. On a drumhead by campfire light he penned words that would reinvigorate the struggle and resound through the generations: "THESE are the times that try men's souls. The summer soldier and the sunshine patriot will, in this crisis, shrink from the service of their country; but he that stands by it now, deserves the love and thanks of man and woman. Tyranny, like hell, is not easily conquered; yet we have this consolation with us, that the harder the conflict, the more glorious the triumph."

As yet, we do not have our own pamphleteer for these soul-trying times. But we still have Thomas Paine's ever-timely words. We do not yet have a writer who can as magnificently express our outrage that a man whose character Paine would deplore is about to become president after losing the popular ballot by nearly 3 million votes. We do not yet have a writer to encourage us to not only resist the ambitions of both the man who would be king and his Tory allies in Congress, but also to turn our outrage into a sustained struggle that will fulfill the promise of democracy. Nonetheless, we have the words that burned like fire in the breast of a man who believed that to be an American in his time meant being a radical.

Really, who better to rally us than this former corset maker, privateer and tax collector who came to America for a second chance in life and gave away all his royalties on a little book that was to become one of the biggest bestsellers in American history so that Washington's army could be outfitted with mittens? Who better to call us out against a royal wannabe who lives in a palatial gilded tower named after himself, proudly boasts that he essentially pays no taxes (while refusing to release his tax returns) and after swearing to "drain the swamp," proceeds to fill it with bottom feeders — a cohort of billionaires, ideologues and cronies he has privileged to dismantle the very government they loathe?

Indeed, who better to mobilize our opposition than the immigrant writer who first envisioned true American greatness and projected achieving it by creating a nation committed to freedom, equality and democracy? "We have it in our power to begin the world over again," he wrote. "A situation, similar to the present, hath not happened since the days of Noah until now. The birthday of a new world is at hand, and a race of men, perhaps as numerous as all Europe contains, are to receive their portion of freedom from the events of a few months."

Relish Paine's attacks on kings and would-be monarchs. Delight in his belief that working people can govern themselves. Listen as he embraces America's ethnic and religious diversity. And note well his plans for establishing an inclusive, prosperous and expansive American democracy.

Pick up Paine's writings and prepare for Inauguration Day by immersing yourself in them. They remain as relevant today as when he wrote them, as Washington's army shivered in the coldest of winters while waiting to once again do battle with the British and their mercenaries.

Carry his works with you. Give copies to friends and family. Read them aloud just as yeomen farmers, artisans, and merchants did in the fields, workshops and taverns of 1776. Drink deeply from his *Common Sense*. Relish his attacks on kings and would-be monarchs. Delight in his belief that working people can govern themselves. Listen as he embraces America's ethnic and religious diversity. And note well his plans for establishing an inclusive, prosperous and expansive American democracy.

Then, when you once again hear Donald Trump revealing, and reveling in, his own ignorance, denying the truth of things and lying practically every time he opens his mouth, recall Paine's observation: "Men who look upon themselves born to reign, and others to obey, soon grow insolent; selected from the rest of mankind their minds are early poisoned by importance; and the world they act in differs so materially from the world at large, that they have but little opportunity of knowing its true interests, and when they succeed to the government are frequently the most ignorant and unfit of any throughout the dominions."

Then take to heart Paine's adage: "Of more worth is one honest man to society and in the sight of God, than all the crowned ruffians that ever lived."

When Trump talks of banning Muslim immigration and compelling Muslims to register with the authorities, heed Paine's warning that "Suspicion is the companion of mean souls, and the bane of all good society." Recite determinedly these words: "For myself, I fully and conscientiously believe, that it is the will of the Almighty, that there should be a diversity of religious opinions among us."

And when he announces he's going to build walls, institute mass deportations, and deny refuge to refugees, proclaim, as Thomas Paine did, "O ye that love mankind! Ye that dare oppose, not only the tyranny, but the tyrant, stand forth! Every spot of the world is overrun with oppression. Freedom hath been hunted round the globe. Asia, and Africa, have long expelled her. Europe regards her like a stranger, and England hath given her warning to depart. O! receive the fugitive, and prepare in time an asylum for mankind."

As the Tories in Congress and state legislatures around the country move against the democratic achievements of generations – Social Security, the National Labor Relations Act, Medicare and Medicaid, the Affordable Care Act, the Civil Rights and Voting Rights Acts, consumer protections and a woman's right to choose – stand up and pronounce the very words that Washington's troops heard as they boarded longboats and crossed back over the icy Delaware to surprise and defeat the King's troops at Trenton: "Let it be told to the future world, that in the depth of winter, when nothing but hope and virtue could survive, that the city and the country, alarmed at one common danger, came forth to meet and to repulse it."

Let them call us rebels, for we are all the heirs of Thomas Paine.

17

Who Says It Can't Happen Here?

Published at Moyers and Company on February 27, 2017

Donald Trump's candidacy and now, presidency, have resurrected a public discourse not heard in this country since the Great Depression — an anxious discourse about the possible triumph in America of a fascist-tinged authoritarian regime over liberal democracy. It's a fear Sinclair Lewis turned into a 1935 bestselling novel, *It Can't Happen Here* — although, as Lewis told it, it sure as hell *could* happen here.

It did not happen, however. Not then, at least. Electing Franklin Roosevelt as president and taking up the labors of the New Deal, our parents and grandparents not only rejected the sirens of authoritarianism, they actually extended and deepened American freedom, equality and democracy. They subjected big business to public account and regulation; expanded the nation's public infrastructure and improved the environment; empowered the federal government to address the needs of working people and the poor; mobilized farmers' organizations, labor unions, consumer campaigns and civil rights groups and fought for their rights, broadening the "We" in "We the People."

Undeniably, they left a great deal to be done. But they gave themselves the wherewithal to defeat fascism overseas and learned how to democratically rebuild the nation.

Now we find ourselves anxiously asking, *Can it happen here?* Trump has given us plenty of reason to worry. He has referred to Mexican immigrants as murderers and rapists; ordered mass deportations of the undocumented by resorting to what he himself describes as "a military operation";spoken of creating a "Muslim registry" and sought to ban Muslims from entering the country. What's more, he repeatedly has expressed admiration for Russia's authoritarian strongman Vladimir Putin; called members of the federal judiciary "so-called judges"; and charged the news media with being "the enemy of the people." He lost the popular vote but claims it was due to voter fraud and he has proceeded to "govern" as if he actually won a popular mandate. And his Cabinet appointments signal a determination to carry out a decidedly reactionary policy agenda long championed by the right wing.

Not for nothing did Senator John McCain (R-AZ) tell NBC News's Chuck Todd that we must be wary of our new president: "When you look at history, the first thing that dictators do is shut down the press... And I'm not saying that President Trump is trying to be a dictator. I'm just saying we need to learn from history."

Yes, we do. And in that light, we should recognize that as much as Trump's anti-democratic rhetoric and executive orders are driven by his own demagogic nature, they are propelled by four decades of corporate class war, conservative culture war, and neoliberal political economy and public policies intended to roll back the democratic rights and achievements of the 1960s and 1930s — including Social Security, which Trump's own White House budget director has called "a Ponzi scheme."

Recalling the democratic surge and initiatives of the FDR years, the 1960s witnessed a dramatic renewal of campaigns and legislation to make real the promise of equality and the right to life, liberty and the pursuit of happiness – including for the poor. Pushed by the new democratic activism and inspired by New Deal precedents, President Lyndon Johnson called for the making of a Great Society and a War on Poverty. A liberal-led Congress moved to enhance American democratic life and enrich the public good. To guarantee civil and political equality, Congress passed historic civil rights, voting rights and fair housing acts and, eschewing racial and religious discrimination, enacted a major reform of the nation's immigration law. To combat poverty, they made health care a right for the elderly and poor and expanded educational opportunities for children and young people. To assure citizens healthier and safer lives, they instituted laws and created agencies to clean up and make secure the environment, marketplace and workplace. *And* to advance the Founders' democratic vision of an informed, culturally aware and historically conscious citizenry, they established the Corporation for Public Broadcasting (subsidizing, in part, PBS and NPR) and the National Endowments for the Arts (NEA) and Humanities (NEH).

In those same years, the Supreme Court extended and deepened the reach of the Bill of Rights by reinforcing the wall of separation between church and state, strengthening the rights of the accused, and acknowledging the right of privacy for women exercising responsibility over their own bodies. And many a state legislature north and west expanded industrial democracy by granting collective bargaining rights to public workers.

Yes, urban rioting and anti-war protests divided our citizens and often overshadowed democratic advances. Nevertheless, Americans had initiated a "rights revolution" and once again enlarged both the "We" in "We the People" and the powers of the people. In the background you could hear echoes of FDR's famous speech on "The Four Freedoms."

The democratic surge of the long 1960s terrified not only white supremacists in Dixie and political and religious conservatives and reactionaries nationally, but also corporate chiefs and executives. They bristled at regulations from federal agencies old and new, and at paying taxes for government programs and "entitlements" (as well as a war in Southeast Asia). They felt threatened by labor unionists, movements of women and people of color, public-interest groups and an "adversary culture" of students, the media, and "value-oriented" scholars and intellectuals. At the same time, US companies were experiencing a "profits squeeze" due to foreign competition, and an oil crisis was contributing to economic "stagflation." So business leaders called for concerted action against what they saw as "an excess of democracy" that urgently needed subduing. Organized in such groups as the National Association of Manufacturers, the Chamber of Commerce, the Trilateral Commission, and the Business Roundtable, corporate executives mobilized in every way to reverse the democratic tide.

Meanwhile, ultra-rich magnates like the Coors and Koch brothers, along with the richly endowed Bradley and John M. Olin foundations, funded efforts to mobilize Christian evangelicals around "culture war" questions like school prayer and abortion and white working people around mantras of law and order and tax reduction.

The last was most appealing. As companies moved operations and jobs first south and then overseas, as unionism took a beating, and as wages were frozen or reduced and benefits were cut, voting for politicians who promised to lower taxes seemed an attractive option for many workers, few of whom realized that the greatest tax cuts would go to the very rich.

Liberal and progressive forces sought to defend and advance past democratic achievements, but Democratic President Jimmy Carter turned his back on the legacy of FDR, LBJ, and those we would come to call the Greatest Generation. Paving the way for the New Right Republican presidency of Ronald Reagan and the age of neoliberalism, Carter abandoned the liberal agenda of labor, environmentalism and consumer rights in favor of cutting government programs, lowering taxes and deregulating capital.

Republicans moved right, and under Bill Clinton, the Democrats followed suit. Liberals and progressives scored occasional victories, especially regarding equal rights for gays and lesbians, but corporate and conservative reaction steadily advanced against freedom, equality and democracy.

In state after state, conservatives have acted to override or circumvent a woman's right to choose by enacting laws intended to make abortions almost impossible to secure. In state after state, Republicans have sought to suppress the votes of people of color, the poor and students by enacting voter ID laws. After years of trying, they finally succeeded by way of *Shelby County v. Holder* (2013) in getting a conservative Supreme Court to disembowel the Voting Rights Act of 1965. *And in state after state,* the corporate and conservative rich have smashed labor unions and effectively suppressed the voices of workers by enacting so-called right to work laws — even, as in Wisconsin in 2011, rescinding the collective bargaining rights of public employees. Who now speaks of industrial democracy?

But Republicans have had no monopoly on subverting democracy and the rights of working people. When and where were workers and environmental activists heard when the Clinton administration negotiated NAFTA and the Obama administration negotiated the now derailed TPP – which Obama saw as central to his "legacy"? When and where were the American people brought into the conversation when the Obama White House negotiated the Affordable Care Act with Big Pharma and the health insurance industry, accepting concessions that would come home to haunt the early successes of the act? And let's not forget that it was not only Senate Republicans who voted for the Bush administration's USA Patriot Act in 2001, a law that has critically threatened the privacy of US citizens. Only one Democratic senator dissented, Wisconsin's Russell Feingold.

We have endured nothing less than 40 years of *creeping authoritarianism* — and it now appears that it may run right over democracy. Jeff Sessions as attorney general — despite having once been denied a federal judgeship because of his racist proclivities — augurs nothing but ill for civil rights and voting rights. Tom Price as Secretary of Health and Human Services signals efforts to privatize Medicare and even Social Security. And Betsy DeVos as Secretary of Education promises to speed up the transfer of dollars from public to private and parochial schools. Thrilling the Republican right all the more, the Trump administration wants to defund the Legal Services Corporation, which provides "financial support for civil legal aid to low income Americans," the Corporation for Public Broadcasting, and the NEA and NEH.

Revealing their authoritarian inclinations all the more, right-wing Republican legislators in several states are introducing bills to criminalize protest activities — and, in Iowa, for example — to require that only Republicans be appointed to university faculties.

Roosevelt warned us of what might happen if we did not sustain the "march of democracy." In a radio address on the eve of the 1938 congressional mid-term elections, with authoritarianism on the rise globally and conservative and reactionary forces in America organizing anew, he said:

As of today, Fascism and Communism — and old-line Tory Republicanism — are not threats to the continuation of our form of government. But I venture the challenging statement that if American democracy ceases to move forward as a living force, seeking day and night by peaceful means to better the lot of our citizens, then fascism and communism, aided, unconsciously perhaps, by old-line Tory Republicanism, will grow in strength in our land.

The Fight for $15, the Moral Monday Movement, the anti-fracking and block-the-pipelines campaigns, Black Lives Matter, and the popular enthusiasm for Bernie Sanders's run for the 2016 Democratic nomination indicated that Americans were, after many years, reinvigorating the nation's democratic pulse. And both Hillary Clinton's popular vote victory and the massive turnout across the United States for the Women's March on inauguration weekend make clear that our resistance is a movement of the majority.

But the resistance must be about more than Trump. The democratic energies we expressed in the years and months leading up to November 2016 must lead to a struggle *for* democracy, which means a sustained struggle against the authoritarianism of both Trump and the reactionary forces that enabled his rise to power and authority. We must resist the future now taking shape in the fevered imagination of those like chief White House strategist Steve Bannon, who once openly admitted to emulating Lenin in wanting to "destroy the state" and wants to push us further and further to the right.

The die is cast. To secure American democratic life, we must resist and overcome not only the initiatives of the greedy, corrupt, bigoted and narcissistic bully who currently occupies the White House, but also the anti-democratic ambitions and schemes of corporate capital and the right. If our parents and grandparents' lives tell us anything, it is that it's not just a matter of rejecting authoritarianism but of acting in solidarity to radically enhance freedom, equality and democracy.

18

We Are Radicals at Heart – Don't Forget It!

I delivered this speech as the Keynote Address to the Wisconsin League of Women Voters Annual Convention on June 9, 2017. It was published by Moyers and Company on June 30, 2017. I have revised it slightly for this volume.

Listen. Listen closely to Thomas Paine's argument in *Common Sense* that "We have it in our power to begin the world over again"; to the Founders' phrases in the Declaration of Independence: "We hold these Truths to be self-evident, that all Men are created equal, that they are endowed by their Creator with certain unalienable Rights, that among these are Life, Liberty and the Pursuit of Happiness–That to secure these rights, Governments are instituted among Men, deriving their just powers from the Consent of the Governed;" to the Framers' first three words of the Preamble to the Constitution, "We the People."

Listen well. Listen well to Abraham Lincoln speaking at Gettysburg in 1863: "[T]hat this nation, under God, shall have a new birth of freedom; and that government of the people, by the people, for the people shall not perish from the earth"; to Franklin Roosevelt telling his fellow citizens in 1936 that "This generation of Americans has a rendezvous with destiny" and calling on them just a few years later to fight for "Freedom of speech and expression... Freedom of worship... Freedom from want... Freedom from fear"; *and* to Martin Luther King Jr. sermonizing on the steps of the Lincoln Memorial in 1963: "I still have a dream... I have a dream that one day this nation will rise up and live out the true meaning of its creed..."

Those are not just memorable words. They are revolutionary, radical, *democratic* words – words that at critical times proclaimed, affirmed, and articulated anew America's revolutionary purpose and promise – words that charged and recharged American life with radical imperative and democratic impulse – words inspired by and inspiring of the democratic labors and struggles of generations – words empowered by and empowering of grand democratic transformations.

And those words speak to you, don't they?

They speak to us as Americans because we still believe in the nation's promise, we continue to feel that imperative and impulse, we too yearn to transform the nation.

They speak to us as Americans because – for all of our faults and failings, for all of the oppression and tragic contradictions that have marked our history, *and* for all of the many efforts by the powers that be to have us think otherwise of ourselves – we are radicals at heart.

The time has come to recognize it. The time has come to embrace our radical history – indeed, *to take hold of that history* – and to make America radical once again.

We were ready to make history anew in 2016 – and in a most tragic way we did. We gave conservatives and reactionaries control of both houses of congress and, by way of the Electoral College, elevated to the presidency a man who represented not "the better angels of our nature," but the worst. And yet, it might have been otherwise.

After more than forty years of corporate class war, conservative political ascendance, and neoliberal public policies that together had subordinated the public good to private greed, laid siege to the hard-won rights of workers, women, and people of color, enriched the rich at the expense of everyone else, hollowed out the nation's industries and infrastructures, breached the wall separating church and state, taken us into catastrophic military engagements, produced a devastating recession and lethargic recovery, and pushed the environment to the brink, we were stirring politically.

After more than forty years of widening inequalities, intensifying insecurities, and mounting injustices, more and more of us were coming to realize that our political and economic elites had trumped democracy with plutocracy, sequestered the nation's historic purpose and promise, and ripped off the American dream. We recognized the crisis we faced, and we were rejecting the narratives of the Republican and Democratic establishments. We were rejecting narratives that had bolstered corporate ambitions, empowered the right to take complete control of the Party of Lincoln, and enabled neoliberals to both drive the progressive spirit of FDR out of the "People's Party" and subject that party to the Money Power – narratives that had led us to ignore or repress our deepest democratic impulses – narratives that had led us to deny who we are.

We expressed it first in the Wisconsin Rising and Occupy Wall Street movements. Our marches and occupations ended in defeats, but the chants of *"This is what democracy looks like!"* continued to reverberate and the energies they excited soon came back to life in the Fight for $15, the anti-pipeline campaigns, the Dreamers and immigrant rights struggles, the Chicago Teachers' strike, the North Carolina Moral Monday movement, and Black Lives Matter, and the enthusiasm for Elizabeth Warren's calls to corral the big banks and financial institutions. Finally, we shook up the two major parties when millions of us turned out to vote for either Senator Bernie Sanders's "Political Revolution" or real-estate mogul and dealmaker Donald Trump's "Make America Great Again."

After more than forty years of acting like deer caught in headlights – the headlights of history – we were moving once again. Moving to renew American democracy, redeem America's promise, and reclaim the American dream. In fact, ever swelling numbers of us actually said we wanted *radical* action to address the crisis. And yet, as the 2016 elections tragically revealed, we remained sorely divided over what that should entail. We were rejecting the narratives that had both cloaked and enabled class war from above, but we had yet to cultivate one of our own.

We needed a story that would enable us to remember who we are and what that demands – a story that would engage our shared anxieties and longings, encourage our renascent hopes and aspirations, and empower our resurgent energies and agencies – a story that would remind us that we are radicals at heart and that to truly "make America great again" we must enhance freedom, equality, and democracy, not diminish them. But we didn't get it.

The time has come to take hold of our history, our truly radical history. The history of how a generation of Americans came to recognize they had it in their power to "begin the world over again" and proceeded to not only turn their colonial rebellion into a war for independence and the making of a democratic republic, but also imbue American life with radical imperative and democratic impulse by declaring a revolutionary promise of freedom, equality, and democracy for all. The history of how generations of evangelicals, freethinkers, workingmen's advocates, abolitionists, suffragists, labor unionists, agrarian populists, socialists, progressives, fighting liberals, environmentalists, and equal rights activists served as the prophetic memory of that promise *and* how generations of ordinary men and women struggled to make real the right to "life, liberty, and the pursuit of happiness" and to expand not only the *We* in We the People, but also the powers of the people. *And most especially today*, the history of how our greatest generations confronted mortal crises and enemies in the 1770s, 1860s, and 1930s and 1940s, not to mention the 1960s, and prevailed over and against them not by suspending their finest ideals but by making America radically freer, more equal, and more democratic than ever before.

History may seem an extravagance in view of the crisis we face. But history, narrative, memory matter – powerfully so. As political scientist Benjamin Barber once put it, "The story we tell about ourselves defines not just us but our possibilities." Or as historians Joyce Appleby, Lynn Hunt, and Margaret Jacob wrote in 2004: "Narratives and meta-narratives are the kinds of stories that make action in the world possible. They make action possible because they make it meaningful." Or indeed, as essayist Wilson Carey McWilliams observed in that ominous sounding year of 1984: "As Orwell knew, a people's memory sets the measure of its political freedom."

Our political and economic elites have always understood that. And ever anxious about – if not downright fearful of – our democratic impulses, they have been ever eager to suppress, marginalize, and if necessary and possible, appropriate histories that might encourage those energies and to promulgate those that would serve to discharge, deter, corrupt, or at least discourage them – which is no easy task in a nation created in a democratic revolution and enhanced by generations of democratic struggles and transformations.

In the wake of the democratic upsurge of the 1960s, which led to the enactment of civil rights laws, major immigration reform, antipoverty programs such as Medicare, Medicaid, and Head Start, *and* laws protecting the environment, consumers, and workers, corporate leaders mobilized. Fearing the formation of a broad democratic left determined to not only reinvigorate that surge, but also radically transform the nation all the more as a progressive New Deal coalition had in the 1930s, they declared war on what they called an "excess of democracy." And with progressive public-interest groups, the movements of labor, women, and the poor, *and* the liberal media and academics who were asking critical questions about past and present in their sights, they organized new associations and lobbying efforts; hired teams of lawyers to combat activism and bust unions;

underwrote think-tank "scholars" to counter the arguments of journalists and professors; launched massive pro-corporate public relations and advertising campaigns; *and* invested ever more heavily in pro-business politicians.

Doing so, they paved the way for the conservative and neoliberal takeovers of the Republican and Democratic parties, respectively. And ever since, "New Right Republicans" and "New Democrats" have wielded the powers of the past to circumscribe, shape, and direct American historical memory and imagination.

Determined to stymie progressive energies and undo or undermine the liberal and social-democratic achievements of not just the 1960s, but also those of the 1930s, conservatives, led by actor-turned-politician Ronald Reagan, made the use and abuse of the past a hallmark of their campaigns and his presidency. In 1980, candidate Reagan spoke directly to the fears and frustrations engendered by energy crises, defeat in Vietnam, the Watergate scandal and President Nixon's resignation, "economic stagflation," and the 1979 Iran hostage crisis. Lambasting the Carter Administration and the Democrats for their failure to act effectively and inspire confidence, he conjured up nostalgic images of a lost America: a stand-tall America ready to assert its interests abroad; a virtuous and prosperous America peopled by hard-working families and school-praying children; a "Shining City on a Hill" America undisturbed by assassinations, urban riots, and student protests and uncorrupted by big government, high taxes, regulatory agencies, welfare programs, affirmative action, and women's liberation. And promising to "make America great again," he gathered together an electoral coalition of corporate executives, Main Street business owners, Christian evangelicals, conservative, libertarian, and neoconservative intellectuals, *and* rightwing special interest groups such as the National Rifle Association.

Accepting the Republican nomination, Reagan, a one-time

FDR Democrat, proclaimed what the media dubbed the "Reagan Revolution" by poaching the words of popular heroes of the left and working people: Thomas Paine's "We have it in our power to begin the word over again;" Abraham Lincoln's "new birth of freedom;" and Franklin Roosevelt's "this generation has a rendezvous with destiny." No less audaciously, he hijacked the Founders, the Stars and Stripes, and the idea of American exceptionalism to the right, stripped them of their revolutionary and radical lives, histories, and meanings, *and* refashioned them as the champions, symbol, and vision of limited government, private enterprise, and a faith-based nation.

Recognizing the esteem in which Americans hold the "Founding Fathers," Reagan zealously crafted a narrative of a divinely-ordained America that they had made exceptional by proclaiming a promise of "individual liberty and freedom" – a narrative in which Americans had rejected the "big government" of the British Crown in 1776 and were now resisting those of not only both Soviet communism and European socialism, but also New Deal and Great Society liberalism – a wondrous narrative that utterly ignored both the contradictions between the nation's ideals and realities past and present *and* the democratic struggles then and since to make real those ideals.

Even as Reagan urged Americans to remember their history and pass it on to their children, he himself did more to suppress it than sustain it. In a convocation address at his college alma mater in February 1984, Reagan – who that very June would speak movingly of the American GIs who fought the Second World War at events commemorating the 40th anniversary of the D-Day Normandy landings – actually denigrated the achievements that their generation, the Greatest Generation, his own generation, had secured by electing FDR and harnessing the powers of government to fight the Great Depression, pursue the War Effort, create postwar American prosperity, *and* enact the democratic reforms of the 1960s: "In the depression years and their aftermath, we forgot the first founding lesson of the American Republic: that without proper restraints, government the servant becomes quickly the master... In the past half century, America has had its flirtation with statism, but we're now returning to our roots: limited government, the defense of freedom, faith in the future and in our God."

Democratic Presidents Jimmy Carter, Bill Clinton, and Barack Obama offered no real challenge to the right-wing storytelling. Carter actually pioneered the "Reagan Revolution." Declaring that "government cannot solve our problems" – which Reagan himself would cleverly outdo with "Government is not the solution to our problems; government is the problem" – Carter abandoned his promises to the labor and consumer movements, turned his back on the Democratic tradition of FDR, and pursued policies of "national austerity" and corporate deregulation.

Twelve years later, Clinton followed suit. Betraying the labor and environmental movements, he pushed the pro-corporate North American Free Trade Agreement (NAFTA) through Congress and – after declaring "the era of big government is over" – signed off on deregulating the communications industry, initiating "mass incarceration," ending "welfare as we know it," *and* killing the New Deal law prohibiting commercial banks from undertaking risky investment banking activities (which paved the way to the Great Recession of 2009).

Moreover, Clinton, like Reagan, told a story devoid of democratic struggles. Taking office in January 1993, William Jefferson Clinton did his best to identify himself with the Revolutionary author of the Declaration, Thomas Jefferson. After retracing Jefferson's inaugural trek from Monticello to Washington to take the oath of office, Clinton delivered an Inaugural Address replete with Jeffersonian references. But the way Clinton presented the Founder and third President revealed his own elitist dread of democratic energies and apparent desire to keep "the people" passive and far from power. Calling on

Americans to "be bold, embrace change, and share the sacrifices needed for the nation to progress," Clinton stated: "Thomas Jefferson believed that to preserve the very foundations of our nation, we would need dramatic change from time to time." And yet, as Clinton surely knew, Jefferson did not say we needed simply *change* to sustain the Republic. He said, "I hold that a little *rebellion* now and then is a good thing, and as necessary in the political world as storms in the physical."

The new President's historical revisionism was telling. His 1993 Task Force on National Health Care Reform, headed by Hillary Clinton, operated behind closed doors and – even as Republicans and the health insurance industry were doing everything they could to bury "Hillarycare" before the plan was ever released – William Jefferson Clinton made no effort to rally Americans to fight for it.

Obama's and the Democrats' victories in 2008 actually seemed to promise a *new* New Deal to combat the deepening Great Recession and address America's widening inequalities. And yet after signing into law massive economic stimulus bills and a major healthcare act (though notably, a most corporate friendly one), Obama too moved in a decidedly neoliberal direction. Preaching the need for government "to live within our means... just like responsible families and businesses do," he created a National Commission on Fiscal Responsibility and Reform in 2010 and named two "budget hawks" to co-chair it. Hoping to cut a deal on reducing the deficit with the now Republican-dominated Congress, he even announced his readiness to "put everything on the table" – including Social Security and Medicare. And breaking his promise to labor and working people that he would march with them in solidarity, Obama not only kept his distance from the Wisconsin Rising of 2011, but also pressed hard for enactment of the ultimately-doomed Trans-Pacific Partnership.

Rallied by his words *"Yes We Can!"* Americans might well

have imagined that Obama would muster them for a fight against the forces that had led them into the recession. But he did not. When he spoke as President he usually drained human agencies from his histories. Delivering his First Inaugural Address in the shadows of the intensifying economic crisis, he made no reference to corporate capital's forty-year-long class war from above and what it had wrought. Instead, he held all Americans accountable for the crisis: "our economy is badly weakened, a consequence of greed and irresponsibility on the part of some, but also our collective failure to make hard choices and prepare the nation for a new age." And when he was finally compelled to address the nation's ever-widening inequalities, he repeatedly cited technological change and globalization as the culprits – not conservative politics, corporate decision-making, and union busting.

Moreover, whereas before becoming President, Obama had spoken appreciatively of how radical and progressive movements had fought to realize "America's Promise" and, when threatened, "to keep it alive," he now showed little inclination to do so. In that First Inaugural Address, he presented a narrative of "American greatness" that disregarded democratic struggles: "it has been the risk-takers, the doers, the makers of things... who have carried us up the long, rugged path toward prosperity and freedom."

Similarly, while Obama referred often and proudly to his Greatest Generation grandparents, he related a Reaganesque tale of how their generation created America's postwar prosperity that completely overlooked the democratic labors, struggles, and investments which made it all possible. As he told the crowd at Osawatomie High School in Kansas on December 6, 2011: "They believed in an America where hard work paid off, and responsibility was rewarded, and anyone could make it if they tried — no matter who you were, no matter where you came from, no matter how you started out. And these values gave rise to the largest middle class and the strongest economy that the world has ever known."

Scholars and critics have debunked and deconstructed conservatives' and neoliberals' uses and abuses of the past. But debunking is not enough and on its own can even be counterproductive, if not cynicism inducing. Apparently haunted by the worst of our national experience, liberal and progressive politicians have essentially compounded America's historical tragedies by turning their backs on not just the betrayals of America's promise, but also the inspiring and compelling story of the struggles to advance it – which has effectively inhibited the making of a progressive narrative and ceded the idea of American exceptionalism to the right.

The 2016 presidential campaigns, for all of their originality, in a certain fashion *perverse* originality, actually mimicked those of the recent past. The candidates of the party of conservatism and reaction not only parroted Reagan's "history" as dogma and his rendition of American exceptionalism as a mantra (which the GOP placed right up front in its party platform). They also promulgated a nostalgic past intended to exploit and exacerbate Americans' divisions, suspicions, and fears. Meanwhile, those of the party of liberalism and progressivism advanced no narrative whatsoever.

Making Ronald Reagan's "Make America Great Again" his own campaign slogan, Donald Trump followed Reagan in conjuring up an image of a "lost America" – an America powerful, secure, and ever growing with booming industries, lots of well-paying jobs, and a thriving middle class – a safe and orderly America that left out, yet clearly alluded to, the racism and sexism of "those days" – an America before Muslim refugees and millions of undocumented Mexican immigrants.

But did we hear another story from the Democrats? Even as they were eschewing decades of neoliberalism in response to our rising anger and activism, did they speak of how "the America" that Trump and Company were promising to restore was created by regulating capital, taxing the rich, empowering workers, *and* investing heavily in not only the public works and initiatives of the New Deal and the War Effort, but also a generation of young Americans by way of the GI Bill?

Even as we were stirring as we had not stirred in decades, did they evoke America's revolutionary promise, recall our radical tradition, or seek to connect struggles past and struggles present in favor of empowering our democratic resurgence? Did we hear them speak strongly and proudly of the campaigns by workingmen to secure the vote, by evangelicals and freethinkers to guarantee separation of church and state, by abolitionists and slaves to end human bondage, and by labor unionists to organize, gain a voice in industry and secure an American standard of living? Did we hear of the fights by agrarian populists to control or regulate banks and railways; by socialists and progressives to combat plutocracy, corruption, and exploitation; by suffragists to enfranchise women; by feminist, labor, civil rights, and gay activists for justice and equality; *and* by consumer and environmental activists to enhance the quality of American life? Did we hear of how those heroic struggles not only made the Declaration's promise of equality and the right to "life, liberty and the pursuit of happiness" all the more real, but also enlarged the We in "We the People" and the powers of the people? Did we hear of how they have made America great, indeed, made America America? At the least, did you ever hear them cite the names or quote the words of Thomas Paine, Frederick Douglass, Walt Whitman, Elizabeth Cady Stanton, Abraham Lincoln, Ida B. Wells, Eugene V. Debs, A. Philip Randolph..?

And even as more and more of us were saying we wanted radical action, did they recount how our greatest generations actually made America great, not exceptional, in the Revolution, the Civil War, the Great Depression, World War II, and the 1960s, by radically enhancing freedom, equality, and democracy? Hell, did they recall how Americans *from the bottom up* pushed George Washington, Abraham Lincoln, and Franklin Roosevelt to go further than they might otherwise have gone... How farmers, artisans, and slaves in their respective ways compelled Washington to declare for Independence and a Republic... How slaves fought to emancipate themselves and empowered Lincoln to issue the Emancipation Proclamation and turn the Civil War into a war of liberation... And how workers, women, and African Americans pressed FDR to advance the New Deal in an ever more social-democratic direction...?

Yes, Bernie Sanders spoke spiritedly of the politics and ideas of Franklin Roosevelt, Lyndon Johnson, and Martin Luther King, Jr. when explaining "democratic socialism" in November 2015 at Georgetown University – and he even made it clear that "we" would have to "turn out" to realize his progressive agenda. But he quickly returned in primary debates and on the campaign trail to highlighting social-democratic Denmark *not* the American social-democratic tradition. And yes, Hillary Clinton launched her campaign at New York's Franklin Roosevelt Four Freedoms Park. But Clinton never actually stated what the Four Freedoms were or ever referred to them again in the course of her campaign – and she sounded more like Bill Clinton than FDR by continually declaring that she wanted to fight *for us* as opposed to encourage the fight *in us*.

We need to take hold of our radical history and make America radical once again. Generations past call on us to do so. Our own historical longings urge us to do so. And Americans yet to come await our determination in doing so. As the Progressive journalist Henry Demarest Lloyd put it more than a century ago: "The price of liberty is something more than eternal vigilance. There must also be eternal advance. We can save the rights we have inherited from our fathers only by winning new ones to bequeath our children."

Take it from the kids.

In September 2014, just months after Colorado school board elections, the now-conservative-dominated Jefferson County Board took up a motion to revise the teaching of Advanced Placement US History. In the words of the Board member who first proposed it: "Materials [for the teaching of US history] should promote citizenship, patriotism, essentials and benefits of the free enterprise system, respect for authority and respect for individual rights. Materials should not encourage civil disorder, social strife, or disregard of the law." And as far as she and her fellow rightwing Board members were concerned, the "AP" US History curriculum was subversive.

The Jefferson County conservatives were not really looking to create a curriculum that promoted American ideals of citizenship and patriotism. Instigated by national rightwing organizations' missives assailing the AP curriculum for failing to highlight "American exceptionalism" and a Republican National Committee resolution which branded it "a radically revisionist view of American history that emphasizes negative aspects of our nation's history while omitting or minimizing positive aspects," they were looking to institute one that would inculcate *conservative* understandings of them – understandings that would deter democratic thinking and discourage dissent. And they were far from alone in trying to do so. Conservatives across the country were ardently pursuing similar initiatives.

Liberals responded by insisting that historical pedagogy should convey both the positive and the negative of America's past. And any good historian would surely agree. But those who would be most affected by the conservatives' motion took more direct action.

Hoping to deter the Board's actions, Jefferson County high school students decided to show their elders what democracy looks like. They not only organized an on-line petition drive that garnered 40,000 signatures, but also came to school dressed as radicals from America's past and walked out of their classes in protest.

Nonetheless, the Board's conservative majority – no doubt all the more convinced that they were doing the right thing – pushed through the "review and revise" policy.

The kids lost the battle. And yet, outfitting themselves with America's radical history, they signaled to us what we must do to start winning it.

Afterword

America needs something more right now than a "must-do" list from liberals and progressives. America needs a different story... the leaders, and thinkers, and activists who honestly tell that story and speak passionately of the moral and religious values it puts in play will be the first political generation since the New Deal to win power back for the people... The right story will set our course for a generation to come...

Tell it – for America's sake.
Bill Moyers, "A New Story for America" (2006)

The time has come. The crisis intensifies and the struggle is joined. Lincoln's warning of 1862 – "We shall nobly save, or meanly lose, the last best hope of earth" – speaks ever more directly to us. But keep listening. Lincoln did not merely issue a warning to his fellow citizens. Believing they already essentially knew what he was to say, he reminded them of who they were and made it perfectly clear to them what they had to do to overcome the crisis and prevail against the enemy they confronted. He told them that winning the war and sustaining the Union required not simply defeating the Confederacy, but also making America's revolutionary promise all the more real for all the more Americans. He told them that to truly secure the United States they had to end slavery. He called on them to make America radically freer, more equal, and more democratic.

The time has come for us to do the same. The time has come for us to remind ourselves of who we are and what that demands. The time has come for us to take hold of our history and make America radical again.

The democratic energies and agencies of the Resistance suddenly manifested in the wake of the November 2016 elections reveal that Americans not only continue both to believe in America's revolutionary promise and to feel the radical impulse imbued in American life by the Revolution and sustained by the struggles of generations, but also yearn to defend American democratic life. Thus, they challenge not only a treacherous and reactionary President and his ever more rightwing Republican party. They challenge us – the democratic left – as well.

They challenge progressives, radicals, socialists, and true liberals to do what we have failed to do for the past forty years. They challenge us to finally fulfill the fearful expectations that drove the corporate powers that be and their conservative and neoliberal champions in the 1970s to declare war on the progress of American democratic life and to pursue to this day class-war and culture-war campaigns against the democratic achievements of generations, the hard-won rights of workers, women, and people of color, *and* the very memory of how those achievements were secured and those rights were won. They challenge us to unite in a "popular front" of the democratic left and work together to not only take back America, but also transform the diverse currents of the Resistance into the kind of broad progressive coalition of democratic forces that capitalists and the right rightly feared. A coalition to liberate the Democratic party – the Party of the People – from the Money Power and take up the fight to truly assure life, liberty, and the pursuit of happiness to all Americans. A coalition determined to not only win elections, but also harness the powers of democratic government, subject capital to ever greater public regulation and control, *and* push the nation all the more in a social-democratic direction.

We cannot delay. We must start doing what we have not been doing. We must embrace our history and recognize that we are radicals at heart. And we must build a coalition of democratic forces which is committed not merely to restoring the democratic legacy of generations and the rights of workers, women, and people of color, but also, if we are to truly secure them, to radically or, if you prefer, *progressively* extending and deepening them. We must address the needs of the commonwealth and its citizens by re-appropriating through taxation the wealth transferred from working people to capital and the rich. We must empower labor both private and public to organize and bargain collectively *and* to elect union brothers and sisters to corporate boards. We must make ourselves more secure by demilitarizing and de-weaponizing everyday American life and by establishing a system of universal national health care. We must enact the Equal Rights Amendment and guarantee a woman's right to control her own body. And we must not simply abolish the Electoral College, but actually enact a constitutional amendment guaranteeing citizens the right to vote.

We must, however, do more than come up with a "must-do list" that will appeal to and draw together diverse interests. We must do what America's finest radical and progressive voices have always done in the face of crises and forces determined to stymie, or bring an end altogether to, the progress of American democratic life. We must recover and proclaim anew the revolutionary promise projected in *Common Sense,* the Declaration, the Preamble, and the Bill of Rights so as to call out the powers that be and call forth our fellow citizens.

We must do what our greatest democratic poet Walt Whitman did on the eve of the Civil War when he wrote in his continuing epic, *Leaves of Grass*:

YOU just maturing youth! You male or female!
Remember the organic compact of These States,
Remember the pledge of the Old Thirteen thenceforward to the
rights, life, liberty, equality of man,
Remember what was promulged by the founders, ratified by The
States, signed in black and white by the Commissioners, and read
by Washington at the head of the army,
Remember the purposes of the founders,—Remember Washington;

Remember the copious humanity streaming from every direction toward America;
Remember the hospitality that belongs to nations and men; (Cursed be nation, woman, man, without hospitality!)
Remember, government is to subserve individuals,
Not any, not the President, is to have one jot more than you or me,
Not any habitan of America is to have one jot less than you or me.

And we must do what Elizabeth Cady Stanton and her colleagues did at Seneca Falls in 1848 when they stated in the *Declaration of Sentiments* that "all men and women are created equal"; what Frederick Douglass did in 1852 when he asked his fellow Americans "What to the slave is the Fourth of July?"; what Lincoln did most eloquently at Gettysburg in 1863 when he projected a "new birth of freedom" to assure that "government of the people, by the people, for the people, shall not perish from the earth"; what Eugene Debs did when he called forth Paine and other radicals and progressives to champion the causes of labor and socialism; what Franklin Roosevelt did in proclaiming the Four Freedoms and envisioning the creation of an Economic Bill of Rights for all Americans; what Martin Luther King, Jr. did when demanding a fulfillment of America's revolutionary promise on the steps of the Lincoln Memorial in 1963; and yes, what the kids in Colorado did in 2014 when they protested the suppression of the past by outfitting themselves in America's radical tradition.

Moreover, we must lay claim to or, better, *reclaim* America's past and – without discounting the terrible tragedies and ironies that have marked the lives of so many Americans – articulate the truly radical story of America, the truly radical story that *is* America. The story of how, in the face of fierce opposition, generations of Americans native-born and newly-arrived, men and women in all their extraordinary diversity, have struggled both to realize the nation's fundamental promise of equality and life, liberty, and the pursuit of happiness *and* to enlarge not only the *We* in We the People, but also the powers of the people. The story of how, for all of our terrible faults and failings, we actually have made America freer, more equal, and more democratic. And we must tell that story in a way that enables us to not only appreciate why we feel the impulses and yearnings we do, but also to recognize and embrace our many and diverse struggles to make real the nation's promise past and present as *ours* not respectively "theirs" alone.

We must articulate a story that, while making no guarantees, enables us to see that redeeming America's revolutionary promise, renewing American democratic life, and reviving the American dream for all Americans demands that we act in solidarity both with each other and with our greatest generations past by radically enhancing American democratic life – by making the United States freer, more equal, and more democratic than ever.

Finally, even as we draw inspiration and encouragement from America's radical story, we should never forget what our forebears never forgot, that the America we seek lies not in the past, but in the future that we are struggling to make. And in that spirit, we should recall, if not publicly recite, lines such as these from Langston Hughes's 1936 poem *Let America Be America*:

> *O, let America be America again —*
> *The land that never has been yet —*
> *And yet must be — the land where every man is free.*
> *The land that's mine — the poor man's, Indian's, Negro's, ME —*
> *Who made America,*
> *Whose sweat and blood, whose faith and pain,*
> *Whose hand at the foundry, whose plow in the rain,*
> *Must bring back our mighty dream again.*
>
> *Sure, call me any ugly name you choose —*

The steel of freedom does not stain.
From those who live like leeches on the people's lives,
We must take back our land again,
America!

O, yes,
I say it plain,
America never was America to me,
And yet I swear this oath —
America will be!

The time has come to take hold of our history and make America radical again. The time has come not merely to take back America, but all the more to make America *America*.

Acknowledgments

I never write a piece without first testing my ideas and assertions in conversation with friends, comrades, and family members – and however they respond, they always help me sharpen my arguments. As a happy consequence, I owe much to many. For their many and diverse contributions to my recent thinking about politics past and present, I warmly thank Thomas LeBien, Sarah Russo, Jon Shelton, Alison Staudinger, Andrew Austin, John Nichols, John Cusack, Alyssa Milano, Peter Morley, Mike Burns, Nomi Prins, Rick Brookhiser, Ken Burchell, David Imler, Christian Emanuel, Catie Bauman, Sid Bremer, Jerry Rodesch, Ron and Suzy Pfeifer, Steve and Suze Lomazow, and Norman Lear.

For enabling me to speak "on-air" or at public events, I thank Jonathan Holloway, Thom Hartmann, John Fugelsang, Nicole Sandler, Dean Obeidallah, Tom Sipos, Matt Tomasetti, Lesley Groetsch, Mary Angela Perna, Rick Smith, Josh Zepps, Ben Mankiewicz, Mark Thompson, R.J. Eskow, Kelly Carlin, Steve Paulson, Sam Edwards, Marcus Morris, Paul Sparrow, Clifford Laube, JoAnne Myers, Robert Pyne, Michael Brooks, Gary Miller, Greg Davis, and Ken Germanson.

And for empowering me to write as a "public intellectual" these past several years, I thank Michael Tomasky of *The Guardian*, Rick Shenkman at History News Network, Lynn Parramore of *New Deal 2.0*, Michael Kazin at *Dissent,* Lucas Wittman and Malcolm Jones of the *Daily Beast*, Isaiah Poole of the Campaign for America's Future, Michael Winship, Theresa Riley, and Kristin Miller of *Moyers and Company*.

Every professor needs educating. For challenging me and making me smile, I send hugs to former UW-Green Bay Democracy and Justice Studies students Paul Ahrens, Tess Schleitwiler, Jason Just, Arthur Sonneland, Zoe Rose Dunk, Andrea Fox,

Chris Parker, Sierra Spaulding, Nate Fiene, Anastasia McCain Coppersmith, Chad Osteen, Vlad Bilyy, and Evan Ash – and to York University graduate student Kirsten Per Andersen.

For believing my words bear repeating, getting me to reduce the possible contents of this volume to a real selection, and making me think anew about what I originally said and might yet say, I thank Zero Books publisher Doug Lain. I have truly relished our editorial meetings via Skype and our podcast-conversations on Zero Squared. Here too, I must give an additional shout out to Michael Brooks for introducing these many chapters and me to Doug.

Family matters most, and I have a special one. For never failing to let me know me what they think (almost always with affection), I once again happily thank, and express my love for, the intrepid editorial team of my life-long partner Lorna and our daughters Rhiannon and Fiona.

This volume is dedicated both to my mentors and friends Bill Moyers and Bernie Weisberger *and* to my "grandboy" Toby Gareth Imler. Thank you, Bill. Thank you for having me on *Moyers & Company* more than once, supporting me in my efforts to cultivate a truly democratic story of America, kidding me regularly about a host of things, *and especially* for sharing both your friendship and your friends with me.

Thank you, dear Bernie. Thank you for your timely, expressive, and informative emails. They are the finest history seminar I have ever attended. Indeed, thank you for sharing with me your insights, exasperations, and "Greatest Generation" memories both historical and personal. You always educate me – and you are wonderful.

Finally, thank you Toby. Thank you for your energy, enthusiasm, and determination. I look forward to the day when you can read these lines. You're an intellect, a builder, an engineer, and a radical in the making. Your grandpa loves you.

CULTURE, SOCIETY & POLITICS

The modern world is at an impasse. Disasters scroll across our smartphone screens and we're invited to like, follow or upvote, but critical thinking is harder and harder to find. Rather than connecting us in common struggle and debate, the internet has sped up and deepened a long-standing process of alienation and atomization. Zer0 Books wants to work against this trend. With critical theory as our jumping off point, we aim to publish books that make our readers uncomfortable. We want to move beyond received opinions.

Zer0 Books is on the left and wants to reinvent the left. We are sick of the injustice, the suffering, and the stupidity that defines both our political and cultural world, and we aim to find a new foundation for a new struggle.

If this book has helped you to clarify an idea, solve a problem or extend your knowledge, you may want to check out our online content as well. Look for Zer0 Books: Advancing Conversations in the iTunes directory and for our Zer0 Books YouTube channel.

Popular videos include:

Žižek and the Double Blackmain

The Intellectual Dark Web is a Bad Sign

Can there be an Anti-SJW Left?

Answering Jordan Peterson on Marxism

Follow us on Facebook
at https://www.facebook.com/ZeroBooks and Twitter at https://twitter.com/Zer0Books

Bestsellers from Zer0 Books include:

Give Them An Argument
Logic for the Left
Ben Burgis
Many serious leftists have learned to distrust talk of logic. This is a serious mistake.
Paperback: 978-1-78904-210-8 ebook: 978-1-78904-211-5

Poor but Sexy
Culture Clashes in Europe East and West
Agata Pyzik
How the East stayed East and the West stayed West.
Paperback: 978-1-78099-394-2 ebook: 978-1-78099-395-9

An Anthropology of Nothing in Particular
Martin Demant Frederiksen
A journey into the social lives of meaninglessness.
Paperback: 978-1-78535-699-5 ebook: 978-1-78535-700-8

In the Dust of This Planet
Horror of Philosophy vol. 1
Eugene Thacker
In the first of a series of three books on the Horror of
Philosophy, *In the Dust of This Planet* offers the genre of horror
as a way of thinking about the unthinkable.
Paperback: 978-1-84694-676-9 ebook: 978-1-78099-010-1

The End of Oulipo?
An Attempt to Exhaust a Movement
Lauren Elkin, Veronica Esposito
Paperback: 978-1-78099-655-4 ebook: 978-1-78099-656-1

Capitalist Realism
Is There no Alternative?
Mark Fisher
An analysis of the ways in which capitalism has presented itself
as the only realistic political-economic system.
Paperback: 978-1-84694-317-1 ebook: 978-1-78099-734-6

Rebel Rebel
Chris O'Leary
David Bowie: every single song. Everything you want to know,
everything you didn't know.
Paperback: 978-1-78099-244-0 ebook: 978-1-78099-713-1

Kill All Normies
Angela Nagle
Online culture wars from 4chan and Tumblr to Trump.
Paperback: 978-1- 78535-543-1 ebook: 978-1-78535-544-8

Romeo and Juliet in Palestine
Teaching Under Occupation
Tom Sperlinger
Life in the West Bank, the nature of pedagogy and the role of a
university under occupation.
Paperback: 978-1-78279-637-4 ebook: 978-1-78279-636-7

Ghosts of My Life
Writings on Depression, Hauntology and Lost Futures
Mark Fisher
Paperback: 978-1-78099-226-6 ebook: 978-1-78279-624-4

Sweetening the Pill
or How We Got Hooked on Hormonal Birth Control
Holly Grigg-Spall
Has contraception liberated or oppressed women?
Sweetening the Pill breaks the silence on the dark side of
hormonal contraception.
Paperback: 978-1-78099-607-3 ebook: 978-1-78099-608-0

Why Are We The Good Guys?
Reclaiming your Mind from the Delusions of Propaganda
David Cromwell
A provocative challenge to the standard ideology that Western
power is a benevolent force in the world.
Paperback: 978-1-78099-365-2 ebook: 978-1-78099-366-9

The Writing on the Wall
On the Decomposition of Capitalism and its Critics
Anselm Jappe, Alastair Hemmens
A new approach to the meaning of social emancipation.
Paperback: 978-1-78535-581-3 ebook: 978-1-78535-582-0

Enjoying It
Candy Crush and Capitalism
Alfie Bown
A study of enjoyment and of the enjoyment of studying. Bown asks what enjoyment says about us and what we say about enjoyment, and why.
Paperback: 978-1-78535-155-6 ebook: 978-1-78535-156-3

Color, Facture, Art and Design
Iona Singh
This materialist definition of fine-art develops guidelines for architecture, design, cultural-studies and ultimately social change.
Paperback: 978-1-78099-629-5 ebook: 978-1-78099-630-1

Neglected or Misunderstood
The Radical Feminism of Shulamith Firestone
Victoria Margree
An interrogation of issues surrounding gender, biology, sexuality, work and technology, and the ways in which our imaginations continue to be in thrall to ideologies of maternity and the nuclear family.
Paperback: 978-1-78535-539-4 ebook: 978-1-78535-540-0

How to Dismantle the NHS in 10 Easy Steps (Second Edition)
Youssef El-Gingihy
The story of how your NHS was sold off and why you will have to buy private health insurance soon. A new expanded second edition with chapters on junior doctors' strikes and government blueprints for US-style healthcare.
Paperback: 978-1-78904-178-1 ebook: 978-1-78904-179-8

Digesting Recipes
The Art of Culinary Notation
Susannah Worth
A recipe is an instruction, the imperative tone of the expert,
but this constraint can offer its own kind of potential. A recipe
need not be a domestic trap but might instead offer escape –
something to fantasise about or aspire to.

Paperback: 978-1-78279-860-6 ebook: 978-1-78279-859-0

Most titles are published in paperback and as an ebook.
Paperbacks are available in traditional bookshops. Both print
and ebook formats are available online.
Follow us on Facebook
at https://www.facebook.com/ZeroBooks
and Twitter at https://twitter.com/Zer0Books